LIFE TOUCHED WITH WONDER

LIFE TOUCHED WITH WONDER

The MIRACLE
of LOVE

FROM THE EDITORS OF READER'S DIGEST

THE READER'S DIGEST ASSOCIATION, INC.
PLEASANTVILLE, NEW YORK

CONTENTS

INTRODUCTION

Men wonder at the height of mountains, the huge waves of the sea, the broad flow of rivers, the course of the stars—and forget to wonder at themselves.

—Saint Augustine

We feel awe when we see a grand landscape or view the majesty of a starry sky. But there's also wonder in a child's kiss when you're feeling down, in a friend's unexpected recovery from a frightening illness, in a walk on a hushed, snowy night. Such moments take us by surprise and lift us from the mundane and familiar. Suddenly, inexplicably, we catch a glimpse of a reality beyond ourselves, and see evidence that there is something beautiful, merciful, loving knit into the fabric of creation—even in ourselves.

In fact, ordinary people can be the most gifted messengers of wonder. Their stories offer compelling evidence of the power of the spirit in daily life. In this new book series we have selected the best of such true-life stories and present them in separate volumes organized around themes.

The stories in *The Miracle of Love* show that true love is, indeed, a miracle: a force beyond human understanding that surprises and transforms us with its elemental power. Whether it comes to us after many years of marriage or in the heady joy of a first kiss, love changes lives, and inspires us to share the best part of ourselves with others.

A HAND TO HOLD

BY

AARON LATHAM

I remember hearing about the Willis girls just before my father's eightieth birthday party. Relatives and friends were coming from thousands of miles away to Spur, Texas, a town of 1300. Among those expected were the Willis girls—four sisters, all in their seventies. They had grown up around Spur but had been gone for a long time. I wasn't sure why my dad was so happy to hear they were coming—or so disappointed when they changed their minds.

Two years after my father's big party, my mother died. They'd been together for 53 years. All through her illness—for almost two months—he stayed with her in the hospital, often 24 hours a day.

A few days after the funeral, my dad and I played golf on Spur's hardscrabble course. On the ninth tee, he surveyed the landscape: scrawny mesquite trees, dying grass, sand, and a tick-ridden jackrabbit.

"It's a pretty, old world," he said.

It was one of the bravest statements I'd ever heard. My dad knew that he had a lot of trials ahead of him—loneliness, an aging body—but it was still a pretty, old world.

Worried about him being alone, I called him once a day after I returned home to New York. Occasionally he mentioned one of the Willis girls—Gussie Lee—who now lived in Sacramento, California. She'd lost her husband, and she and my father, Clyde, had begun to talk on the phone. Their discussions would end with Clyde pressing her to visit. "Someday," she'd say.

It was almost two years before Gussie came back to Spur. Clyde met the flight and studied the passengers with growing disappointment. She wasn't on the plane. She hadn't come. Then she marched right up to him and demanded, "Are you Clyde Latham?"

Startled and suddenly smiling, he admitted: "Why, yes, I am."

They headed for baggage claim. "I'm sorry I didn't recognize you," he said.

"You weren't looking for a little old lady," said Gussie.

"That's the problem. I *was* looking for a little old lady. When none got off the plane, I was stumped."

"Liar."

"Cross my old heart."

They collected her bag and headed for the car. Gussie had deliberately packed for only four days—an excuse for a short visit.

As they drove toward Spur, Clyde kept Gussie laughing with his stories of youthful pranks and Texas goat drives. Soon the rectangular farms gave way to rugged ranch land, canyons, ravines, red earth—and lots of mesquite trees.

"Aren't they pretty?" Gussie said, a new energy in her voice.

The forgotten beauty of West Texas caught Gussie off guard. And something else did too: laughter. She felt that she'd been crying for two years, ever since her Bill died, and now she was laughing. It was water to a parched soul.

The next day Clyde took Gussie sightseeing. "Stop!" Gussie called. "I want to pick some cotton."

Clyde pulled over, and Gussie hopped out and plunged into the cotton. When she was a girl, the burs had cut her hands, but picking this new cotton was fun. She hurried back to the car with her arms full of white fluff.

Gussie and Clyde told each other they would never get married again. He was eighty-four, she was eighty-one, and they were too old for such shenanigans.

The night before she was supposed to leave, Gussie and Clyde settled down in his side-by-side reclining chairs. One last time, he tried to persuade her to stay a little longer.

"I'll stay another week if you'll promise me one thing," Gussie said.

"Anything," Clyde replied.

"Get a girlfriend after I go. You enjoy a woman's company so much."

When Gussie called home to tell her children, they were stunned. They'd never known their mother to outstay her packing before.

Hearing about these developments, I was uneasy. I'd worried about my father being alone, but I also worried about his getting hurt. How would he feel when she went back to California?

Gussie's extra week in Spur passed all too quickly. The evening before her departure, she and Clyde sat holding hands. He had something he wanted to say, but he was a little nervous. He wasn't a shy man; he was just having trouble finding his voice. Eventually it turned up.

"Gussie, I love you," Clyde said.

She was shocked. She hadn't expected him to say that. They should have left romantic love behind them a long time ago. And yet Gussie startled herself when she replied, "I love you too."

They both sat there in a state of wonder.

On my father's first day without Gussie, I called to see how he was doing. I dialed his number, and kept dialing for the next hour and a half, only to get a busy signal. Finally I got through. "Are you all right?"

"Oh, I was just talkin' to Gussie."

The last time *I'd* talked on the phone like that was when I was in high school. When I called my father the next day, nobody answered. Clyde had caught a flight to Sacramento.

"Gussie, I want to get married," he told her. "Will you marry me?"

"I'll marry you," she said.

On November 1, just a week after my dad had arrived in California, Clyde and Gussie got married. On the plane back to Spur, they chattered away about relatives, each other, their adventure to come.

When they landed, a stranger approached and said, "It's great you two still find each other so interesting. How long have you been married?"

"Three days," Gussie said.

Less than six months after their wedding, Clyde woke up one night with his left foot throbbing. Gussie drove her husband to the hospital, 35 miles away. He was released two days later.

During his second hospitalization, Clyde told the doctor over and over, "I'm worried about Gussie. It's not fair to her. I didn't mean to get her into all this."

Doctors couldn't detect a pulse in his left foot, probably because blood clots were clogging the arteries. They had to be cleaned out or Clyde might lose his leg. Cleaning would mean surgery. Gussie sagged.

That evening I flew in from New York, and the next morning I visited my mother's grave. My father's name was carved on the tombstone with my mother's. Clyde and Gussie had agreed that he would be buried beside my mother, and Gussie eventually would lie next to her late husband, Bill.

Standing there, I recalled my mother's last days in the hospital. My father had stayed with her around the clock. "Don't worry about me," he said. "Save your worry for your mama."

I recalled a phrase that Abraham Lincoln had once used: "the last full measure of devotion." In those final days of my mother's life, my father had given the last full measure of everything that was within him. He had proved his love and devotion completely. Nothing that happened later, not his remarriage, not his new life, could diminish that. My father had earned the right to move on.

Four days after Clyde's surgery, there was still no pulse in his foot. "We're going to have to amputate," said the doctor. Clyde took the news matter-of-factly: "Anyway, maybe it won't hurt anymore."

Early in the morning, Gussie kissed Clyde good-bye. He told her, "You be good now. I hear lots of romances start in hospital waiting rooms." They laughed, and he went through the black doors.

When Clyde woke up, he complained of a terrible pain in his stomach. Once again he was rushed into surgery. Once again Gussie and I spent long hours waiting.

That night, Clyde fought back. I knew it was because of Gussie. If my father hadn't been in love, he would have gone quietly to lie down next to my mother. But he wasn't about to depart this earth now.

The crisis passed, but the next morning Clyde's condition was still grave. Gussie sat there exhausted, trying to put on a bright face.

"How are you?" someone asked.

When you love you wish to do things for. You wish to sacrifice for. You wish to serve.

ERNEST HEMINGWAY

"Oh, I'll be all right," Gussie said. "Don't worry about me."

I began to realize that Gussie was offering her own last true measure of devotion. I hugged her, and she began to cry. I cried too—because I was feeling the happiness that comes out of the sharpest pain.

That was over a year ago—a year of changes for all of us. Recently I flew to Texas for another of my father's birthdays. When I reached his house, I entered through the back door and looked around. They weren't in the kitchen or the living room.

I finally found them in the den, sitting side by side in their recliners, fast asleep, holding hands. It sure was a pretty, old world.

MY ONLY TRUE LOVE

BY

ALBERT DIBARTOLOMEO

My wife and I raced out of Philadelphia as if fleeing a pestilence, only to run into dense shore-bound traffic. We were headed to the coast—a four-day weekend in Stone Harbor, New Jersey, with a stop in Atlantic City.

I have never traveled this route without being flung back to the summers that I spent in Atlantic City during college in the early '70s. There are photos from those years, but I don't need them to prompt trips back in time. The familiar geography alone does the trick.

An hour after leaving Philadelphia, we stood on Sovereign Avenue in the fading light of the June evening. We stopped there to see what had become of the house where I had spent my college summers, working as a busboy in a restaurant in the next shore town south. It was a white wood-frame house of three creaking stories, with a black wrought-iron fire escape attached to its side like an afterthought. I had lived on the third floor.

The house was gone, as were others that had lined the street.

"It's as though it vanished," I said.

8

I gazed upon the profound emptiness in front of me and the ghosts of my past that drifted across it. I pictured myself sitting on the porch leisurely reading novels, lazing on the beach under clear skies, and sprinting to work on my bicycle for the sheer pleasure of feeling the power of my own youthful body.

Then my first love, Jayne, came to mind.

"What are you thinking about?" my wife asked.

"Nothing much. Just those times when I lived here."

I first saw Jayne on an early July morning. I had just begun to clean the front windows of the restaurant, when a girl approached the entrance. I watched her walk through the door. She smiled as our eyes met, and I found myself stammering a hello.

"I'm the new busboy," I said, feeling heat in my face.

"I'm the waitress who's been here too long."

"But it's only a week into the season."

"Exactly." Jayne laughed and went to prepare for the tasks ahead.

Throughout the day I wanted to stop amid the rush of customers to talk to her. Whenever I saw her, my gaze lingered, sometimes into a stare that would have embarrassed me had anyone noticed. In the following days, we began to chat during the midafternoon lull. At first self-conscious and tongue-tied, I was soon talking with a scarcely controllable passion that I had never known before.

Before long, we met on the beach. That afternoon I lay on a blanket with her in a state of near delirium, my breath shortened by her smooth skin glistening in the sun.

On subsequent days we strolled along the Atlantic City boardwalk or sat in the apartment house listening to songs of longing and loss that seemed to speak directly to us. I can no longer remember our conversations, but they were never as important as her mere presence.

I had known other girls, even had a high school sweetheart, but what I felt for them seemed trifling in comparison. This was all-consuming, which is the nature of first love, a sensation felt in our very blood, like intoxication or illness.

About a month after meeting Jayne, I drove her home after a party. Halfway there, it began to storm. The streets became streams, and we moved slowly along in the three-o'clock darkness. Parked outside her house, we sat in the car and talked.

"My heart sometimes jumps when I think of you," I said to her.

She smiled.

"It's true."

Lying in bed some nights, with the whisper of the ocean just reaching me, thoughts of Jayne could literally make my heart skip a beat.

What else could cause that reaction but love? I nearly told her, but it seemed unnecessary in the sweetness of the cocoon around us now, shielding us against the rain.

I left Jayne that night picturing long days ahead spent with her.

But that was the last time we saw each other outside work. A week later Jayne joined me in "our" rear restaurant booth, looking serious.

"What's the matter?"

She paused. "My boyfriend and I are getting back together."

A fist seemed to strike my stomach. "I thought that was over."

"He says that he loves me, and I think I love him too."

I could find nothing to say.

"I'm sorry."

I spent the rest of the afternoon in a daze that barely diminished over the remaining three weeks of summer. I had never in my life felt so hurt, and I thought that I would never recover from it. I felt bitter and angry.

The wound refused to heal. Many months passed, yet there remained a place inside me where Jayne had been that caused me to wince when I touched it.

Then one spring Saturday two years later, I entered a bookstore in Philadelphia and asked a young woman on a ladder where I might find the Shakespeare sonnets I needed for an English class.

She looked down and told me where to find the poetry section. I thanked her, found the volume, and soon left the store.

At the end of my English class a few weeks later, I walked into the hall and saw the bookstore clerk leaving a nearby classroom. I remembered her wheat-colored hair, her warm voice, and intelligent green eyes.

She saw me and smiled in recognition.

"The girl on the ladder," I said when we reached each other.

"The Shakespeare sonnets."

"Do you always remember the books people ask you about?"

"If the people are memorable."

I smiled at that.

We were both heading for other classes, but exchanged names before parting.

I ran into Susan often after that, and we usually said hello or joked and then went on our way. Sometimes we met behind the campus library and sat in the shade of the sycamore trees, talking and loafing. If she failed to show, that was all right. We were just friends passing time, and I preferred it that way. After the anguish of Jayne, I was wary of opening up to anyone.

One afternoon, however, our talk found its way to our parents.

"You would like my mother, I think," I said, "but my father's been dead since I was eleven." I had not intended to mention something that I rarely divulged, even to close friends, and I nearly wished I had kept silent about it.

Susan touched my arm.

"It's been a while," I said.

"I'm still sorry." A darkness crept into her usually bright eyes. "I lost mine at the end of high school."

It was my turn to say that I was sorry.

We sat some long minutes in the slow afternoon, muted by these thoughts. But, I learned then, it was one of Susan's virtues not to allow the wounds that come with life to crowd out the joys, and we were soon talking of more cheerful matters. A few weeks later we began to date.

Saying "I love you"

is a conversation,

not a message.

DOUGLAS STONE

That summer I went to the shore for the final time as a college student. Once a place for adventure and wild excitement, it now seemed little more than a place where I had a guaranteed job. I felt older, wiser, certainly less naïve. And there was a sense of things coming to an end—my youth and the things of youth that we must shed to live stable, responsible lives. This trip was also different in that Susan would occasionally visit on weekends.

Because I worked during the day, we had only the evenings to spend together. The hours felt precious, and we often passed them by the sea merely talking, as though we had stored up what we could not express to others.

Some nights a pathway of moonlight lay across the water, connecting the shore to the horizon. "It's as though we could walk on it," I said once.

"Where would it take us?"

"Wherever we want, I like to think."

"Where would you go?"

"I don't know, but I'd want you to come along."

"Gladly."

We held each other as the night deepened and cooled. It was here, as the waves crashed in the darkness, that I let Susan fully into those guarded places where I'd cloistered my sensitive injuries. She was delicate with them, and as she revealed to me her own secret fears and wishes, I knew what true love was.

After Susan had boarded the bus back to Philadelphia and I was alone, I often wrote to her. She has gathered those letters, yellowing and in a cursive that has changed over the years, in a purse of pink silk at the bottom of an heirloom dresser we received from her mother after we married. I have Susan's letters, too, that I keep in a shoe box. When I read them, I am reminded why I wanted to spend my life with her.

Susan and I rose early in Stone Harbor the following morning and went to the beach to "greet the ocean," as my wife always says. We walked the several blocks in the still cool air and the special hush that comes with mornings by the sea.

"It's so lovely," Susan said, clutching my hand, and I agreed.

Overhead the sea gulls wheeled and cried as we walked barefoot in the cool, wet sand. After a distance, we stopped, and I sat with my back close to a dune, while Susan kept to the shoreline, staring out to sea or looking about for interesting shells or stones. Often she turned and looked at me, the bright early morning sun framing her back.

First love, I thought, may cut and mark us the deepest, but love that lasts and grows does so because it joins and nurtures what is dearest, finest, and noblest in two people. And because it understands and forgives what is less so.

First love may register in the blood with dizzying effect, but the love that endures takes up residence in the soul. In this way, love becomes something far more powerful than bone and flesh. It completes us, gives us the wholeness we need to navigate safely through life.

I could have watched my wife for hours as the waves broke and advanced toward her bare feet. In a world sometimes marred by hurt and anguish, I felt profoundly grateful that the sun had risen for me on such a love. I could feel it now flowing from me to her and back to me again, joined everywhere, complete, like the seas, and a harbor against all tempests.

The best friend is likely to acquire the best
wife, because a good marriage is based on
the talent for friendship.

FRIEDRICH NIETZSCHE

GOLD TOUCHING GOLD

BY

CHRISTOPHER DE VINCK

*F*or the last ten years of her life, my grandmother wore two wedding bands on her finger: hers and my grandfather's. After he died, she carried his memory always warm against her soft, wrinkled hand. This special link of love—gold touching gold—came late in life for them. It happened much earlier for Roe and me, and best of all, it was something we could share.

Following our summer wedding, Roe and I moved into our first home in the late fall. I remember standing on the lawn and thinking, *Wonderful things will happen here in the years to come.* I also thought about the 17 tall oak trees that covered the small yard.

Soon we learned that once a year the township vacuums up and trucks away the leaves raked to the side of the road. But that first year Roe and I, both busy teaching school, missed the collection date. So we would have to rake and bag the leaves, then carry them to the town dump.

The leaves were wet and covered with ice by the time we had a chance to gather them. Roe held the bags open as I scooped up and dropped in the leaves. I didn't have gloves and had to blow into my cold hands.

We raked and raked. One bag, five bags, 15 bags. By the end of the day we had 40 large, leaf-filled plastic bags leaning against the garage.

We entered the house laughing, talking about supper. We walked over to the kitchen sink to wash our hands. That's when I noticed my wedding ring was missing.

"When was the last time you remember having it on?" Roe asked.

"When we were raking the leaves. It must have slipped off then," I answered, feeling very troubled.

Roe and I spent more than an hour bent over the lawn like chickens looking for bits of corn. We glanced at the 40 bags that now seemed like huge wedding-ring-eating elephants.

"We'll have to look through the bags," Roe announced. "We can't take them to the dump today."

"Let's have supper and worry about it tomorrow," I suggested. Deep down, we were concerned and growing more so. Maybe the ring wouldn't turn up in the bags.

The next day was even colder, and the bitter chill spilled into the next week and month. We kept saying, "Tomorrow we'll go through the bags." Life can be like that, tugging us away from what's important.

After three months, the bags were under a foot of snow. One afternoon, when I was still in school, Roe decided to search them for the ring. She lifted the first bag and dragged it across the snow and into the porch at the side of the house.

She opened the bag. Leaves left inside a plastic garbage bag for three months rot. They smell. They turn into a wad of ooze. Roe now picked up a clump of fermenting leaves and sprinkled them around her to sift through the mess. Pebbles, acorns, and sticks bounced against the wood floor. Each time something fell from her hands, she thought, *Perhaps the ring!* No ring.

Roe continued her search. Bag number two. No luck. Bag number three. No luck. Then, after she had jiggled the leaves again and again in bag number four, my wedding ring miraculously popped onto the floor before her startled gaze.

When I came home from work that evening, Roe didn't tell me at first. She simply asked how my day had gone. I asked about hers. We spoke. We laughed. Not until we were preparing for dinner together did I finally notice she was wearing an extra ring on her finger.

"You found it!" I shouted. "I can't believe it!"

Roe took my hand in hers and whispered, "With this ring I thee wed," and she once again slipped it onto my finger—this gold that had now touched gold.

In our life there is a single color, as on an artist's palette, which provides the meaning of life and art. It is the color of love.

MARC CHAGALL

A CURIOUS LOVE STORY

BY

JOSEPH P. BLANK

After the prayers of the minister, the ring of relatives and friends around the twin graves broke up, and the mourners walked slowly away. It was difficult to believe that it was only two days earlier that Kurt and Helga had decided to drive to Erfurt in East Germany to buy black-currant plants for their garden. They had left their four-year-old daughter, Anna, with Kurt's younger brother, Martin. When their car blew a front tire and crashed into a concrete wall, the couple were killed instantly.

Beside the graves, Martin held the sobbing Anna in his arms. The child was frightened and unable to comprehend that she would never see her parents again. Martin stared at her delicate features, narrow face, and tousled blond hair. She looked exactly like her mother at the age of four. Exactly. At that time, 26 years earlier, Martin had seen Helga only for a few minutes, but he vividly remembered that dazed, exhausted expression on her face . . .

Early June was still chilly along the northeast coast of Germany, just south of Denmark. Kurt, fourteen, and Martin, twelve, had permission from their mother to play along a favorite beach, but had been told, "Don't do more than wade, because the water it still too cold." Martin was the more spontaneous and outgoing of the brothers. Kurt was serious, thoughtful, almost taciturn. The one emotion that he expressed without reserve was a compassion for living things in trouble. He was always bringing home a stray dog or an injured bird.

As the boys came to the beach, they saw three young girls waving their arms toward the water and crying. They were the children of Heinz Meier, owner of the biggest farm in the area. Out at sea, bobbing on the swells, was a small yellow rubber boat. In it, barely visible, was four-year-old Helga Meier. The panic-stricken girls said that the dinghy had been pushed out to sea by the strong wind. Their nine-year-old brother had just left to find help.

Kurt said, "It's forty-five minutes to the village. By the time help gets here, she'll be halfway to Denmark." He took off his shirt, trousers, and shoes, and told Martin, "Keep the girls calm." He dashed through the surf and dived into the sea.

Martin had a watch, and now he clocked his brother. It took Kurt 32 minutes to reach the boat. Martin saw him alternately pushing then pulling it toward shore—opposed by a stiff wind. The rescue seemed to take forever. Finally, after an hour and 44 minutes, Kurt was close enough to shore to stand. Martin and the Meier girls splashed in to help. The oldest girl wrapped the frightened child in two sweaters and hurried from the beach. Help from the village had still not arrived.

Kurt collapsed face down on the sand. Martin rolled him over and rubbed him with a dry shirt. His skin was white, his lips were blue. After a few minutes, Kurt asked, "Where's the little girl?"

"They took her home. Are you all right?"

"I think so. I'll just lie here for a while."

On their slow walk home, Kurt told Martin of his ordeal. By the time he had reached the boat, Helga was in water up to her hips. He

didn't climb into the boat for fear of sinking it. A cup attached to a light rope hung from the side; he untied it, then gave it to the child and told her to bail. Clutching the rope, Kurt tried to swim, but made little progress against the rough waves. He put the rope between his teeth and swam backward. When he tired, he swung behind the boat, held on, and kicked hard until he felt able to use his arms again for swimming.

All the while Kurt thought that he and the child would surely drown. But somewhere he found the strength to reach shore.

News of the heroic rescue spread through the village. As congratulations poured in, however, Kurt appeared more and more disconsolate. "He never said a word," recalls his older sister, Iris. "But I knew what was wrong. Old man Meier didn't thank him for saving his daughter. Helga's mother would have, but she was dying in a sanitarium.

"Meier was a hard man, and he never once gave a sign that he even knew Kurt existed. After about a week, Kurt seemed to get over his disappointment. He never again mentioned the rescue."

World War II was now at its height, and Kurt's family moved from their coastal village to Weimar, in the interior of Germany.

The years passed. Iris married. Martin married, too, and had two boys. Kurt became a schoolteacher and remained single. (Martin used to call him *Hagestolz,* or "confirmed bachelor.") He rarely dated or went dancing. His recreation was chess, and he became a top player in the coffeehouses of Weimar. He had a dry sense of humor and an almost cynical attitude, which Iris thought was a disguise to hide his sensitivity.

In 1962—20 years to the summer after the rescue of Helga—Kurt's ailing mother decided to visit relatives in her old home village in what had now become West Germany. Because she was sick and over sixty-five, the East German government granted Kurt a three-day pass to accompany her.

On his second day in the village, Kurt took a walk to the beach where he had rescued Helga. Sitting on a rock staring out to sea, he suddenly realized that he wasn't alone. A tanned, blond young woman with a slim, almost boyish figure was leaning against a nearby tree.

Quite uncharacteristically, Kurt walked over to her. Impulsively, he told her that he had grown up in the village and that this was his first visit in 20 years. They began walking along the beach, shoes in hand. "Look," Kurt said, "my mother is visiting relatives, and I'm bored. Let's go dancing tonight."

She smiled. "Why not?" she replied, almost aggressively. "My name is Helga Meier."

Kurt stopped short. "The little girl in the yellow boat! Twenty years ago. Do you remember? I'm Kurt."

Helga nodded. "I heard that you were in town. I've come down to the beach three times hoping that you would be here. I wanted to thank you." Her expression turned somber. "Don't call for me at the house. I'll meet you at the crossroads."

That evening, Kurt and Helga did no dancing. They talked. Helga was depressed. "I always wanted to thank you," she said. "But I've often wondered whether it might have been better if you hadn't rescued me that morning. I think Meier feels the same way. He believes that my mother was unfaithful. I don't look like his other children, and he has never behaved as if he were my father.

"The rest of the family have followed his lead and treat me like a servant. I do housework and farmwork. I get nothing for it, and Meier keeps telling me that I am illegitimate. I have no one."

Seething inside Kurt was a feeling that he had never before experienced. Holding her hands, he leaned toward Helga and kissed her. "I must leave tomorrow," he told her. "Come with me. Marry me."

She was startled. "But you've known me for only a few hours."

"I know you. I love you."

Then, in a low voice, Helga said, "I like you very much. I think I could love you, but I don't really know." She smiled at Kurt. "Yes, I will go with you. I risk nothing. It is you who are taking the risk."

The next morning, Kurt confronted Meier outside the front door of his big house. He introduced himself—the name rang no bell with Meier—and flatly told the glowering farmer that he was taking Helga to Weimar to marry her.

The news infuriated Meier, but Kurt was adamant. "You can't stop me. It's difficult to get a pass out of East Germany. I am taking Helga with me now."

When you really want love you will find it waiting for you.

OSCAR WILDE

Back in Weimar, an astonished Martin couldn't believe that Kurt—his quiet, cautious bachelor brother—had met, proposed to, and actually carried off a young woman within 24 hours. "And what's even more unbelievable," Martin told his wife, "is that it's *this* girl."

Love was magic for Kurt. His reserve was replaced by spontaneity. He laughed freely. His sense of humor turned from the sardonic to the gentle.

Helga was slower to change. During the first few months she was shy, withdrawn.

Gradually, however, her fears and doubts evaporated. She smiled more—a slow, understanding smile that turned her from pretty to beautiful. The explanation for her change was simple: she had fallen in love with her husband. In two years Helga gave birth to Anna. Kurt was unabashedly proud of his wife and daughter.

The couple were rarely apart. Kurt stopped visiting the coffeehouses where the best chess players gathered; he didn't want to take time from his wife and daughter. He had always disliked working with soil, but when Helga decided to plant a large plot of land, he became an avid gardener and worked at her side. Amazed, Martin told his wife, "I've never seen love change a man so much."

Their love continued to grow. Martin could see it in the way they communicated with a mere touch or glance. Even on social occasions they always sat together. Kurt couldn't keep his eyes off his wife, and Martin once kidded him about it. "I like to watch her," Kurt admitted. "She moves so beautifully, so gracefully."

"Good Lord, you really are in love with your wife," Martin laughed.

Kurt gave his brother a big grin and said, "Forever."

Martin now recalls, "Those were Kurt's best years. And they were the happiest and merriest years for all of us. When Kurt and Helga left, they took a lot of that happiness and merriment with them."

One beautiful summer Sunday, a year before the accident, the two families were in the garden that Helga and Kurt had made. The wives were picking berries; the children were playing; Kurt and Martin sat in the shade of an old, twisted pine tree, relaxed and at peace. Kurt began talking: "You know, before Helga, I really wasn't dissatisfied with my life. I knew what I had, and that was fine with me. But I didn't know what I didn't have.

"Then, Helga! She opened a new world for me. Maybe I did the same for her. She made me know what being alive is, what it means. Now I can't imagine myself without her."

He paused, then said, "Do you believe that some things in life are destined to be? Is it possible? Was it meant for me to save her twenty-five years ago—for myself?"

Love makes that fort yield at night which it
besieged but in the morning; for there is no force
able to resist it.

MIGUEL DE CERVANTES

WHEN LOVE BEGINS AGAIN

BY

JOAN MILLS

The phone rang into the wintry hush of a house where the scent of Christmas still clung. It was Chris, my youngest. "I hope you're sitting down," he said. "Claire just found out—we're going to have a baby this summer!"

A *baby*. I'd be a grandma at last! I could hear Chris chuckling as I said over and over, "Oh, that's wonderful, *wonderful!*"

Yes, he agreed, it was. Then his voice dropped. The timing, as we both knew, was terrible. "We'll manage—we always do," Chris said. "But right now, I can't see how."

Nor could I. Claire was a third-year art student in Maine. Chris, fresh from college, was scouting Boston for a solid base. The interim income from his carpentry was barely keeping them afloat.

It looked like an impossible situation—except that these two are the kind of people you believe in.

"You're not alone with this," I reminded him. "You have two families who love you. And there is something else: having a baby is one of those rare times in life when things you haven't even thought of come into focus and good happens in mysterious ways.

"Chris, I promise you, this will work out—and how it does will amaze you."

"Ma," he replied. "I'm amazed *already!*"

I walked about the house, thinking about Chris, remembering why I believed in him. He was our third, our last, born after a siege of six miscarriages. My spirit had soared to see him safe, and then marveled that he seemed to celebrate his own existence. We gave him a name that sounded to me of all the sweetness, strength, and virtue I could wish for him: John Christian.

His joyful energies outraced any timetable. At three months he was gleefully plunging about the house in a walker. Precociously soon he was up and running into the arms of his big sister, Laurie, or his brother, Bob.

Before he was a year, he made a shambles of six rooms every day, getting himself into unbelievable fixes. But he never broke anything or hurt anybody. He caroled his own songs at the sky and danced with joy for morning. "He always shines!" I said to his dad. "He wears mud as if it were glory."

These days there are educational guidelines and medical treatments to help hyperactive children. Not then. We were on our own with a tiny tornado.

Not surprisingly, he was tossed out of nursery school and kindergarten. But by second grade he was reading two years in advance of his class. In third grade, however, he was expected to sit still; keep his voice down; "behave." Such disciplines were beyond his control.

He was shamed, punished, and labeled. Embattled on the playground by classmates, he fought back. At home he'd crumple, a tear-streaked little boy. We tried private school, clinical review, everything.

No one found a solution. Those were heartbreaking years. School was his private agony.

In high school, though, a friendly faculty kept him in motion. He was stage-struck from the first day of acting class. He played championship soccer, was once vice president of his class. But he graduated woefully aware of his lack of learning, more depressed than almost anybody knew.

Here was a fine, bright boy—intuitive, witty, thoughtful—without a prospect in sight. His dad and I were divorced now, but not from our kids. Chris needed, we thought, time to find his own way. As often before, I said to him, "I believe in you."

He worked in Florida for a while, came home, and hired on as a helper to a crew of young master builders. In their company, his cheer revived.

Evenings, he took a small role in summer stock. During the run of the play, experienced members of the company urged him to go to New York. "You have it in you to be a star," they said. Another in the cast agreed that Chris was talented, but advised, "Get an education first, or you'll miss it all your life."

The first advice dazed him. The second steadied him. He enrolled in prep school in Boston and found that he could sit in the vast public library, reading—and be filled with happiness. He started college. Summers, he rejoined his friends, absorbing the lessons of craftsmanship.

At twenty-two, he fell in love. He walked into a room one night, saw a beautiful girl, and *knew*. Claire saw a handsome boy too shy to speak, and knew too. So did we, when we saw them together.

Chris left school. For two years, they scraped by, feeling rich in time to explore their future. Much alike in their sensitivities, they looked hard at the years ahead before going further.

At length, they determined to complete their education. Of all the sacrifices, the greatest was their separation during the school weeks. This was a statement of faith: someday he'd find a niche in writing or theater; she was clearly meant to be an artist.

And so, on the night Chris called with their news, they had as assets their talents, their devotion, the cheerful courage that had brought them this far—and little else.

Dreading that this fresh financial crisis would force her out of school, Claire had consulted her advisers. She was "too talented to lose," they told her. She was awarded a scholarship, and with it came a surer sense of her creative power.

Chris got a series of carpentry jobs. Suddenly he was busier than he had ever been. His income improved, and he became his own boss. On his nights alone, he wrote for his own pleasure, or went out to see what young performers were up to. Weekends, he and Claire were reunited and recovered their dreams.

Claire was rounding out. With fascination, they felt faint stirrings and wondered *who* was there.

Spring. They had made a strong start. But suddenly it seemed no more than that. Where would they live? In Massachusetts? How would Claire get her degree? In Maine, then? They'd lose the gains Chris had made. How would they furnish a home? What does a baby need?

The children—Laurie and her husband, Joe, Bob and his bride-to-be, Joy, and Chris and Claire—drew closer as a family. Joy's brother suggested that when she and the baby were ready, Claire could earn credits toward graduation by interning at his Boston graphics-design firm. When her advisers agreed, great chunks of the future fell smoothly into place.

Chris was now helping a friend winterize a tiny seaside cottage. At intervals, his friend hinted, "This would be a great place for a couple with a baby—the rent would be reasonable."

"Too small!" Chris always responded. But one morning he watched fishing boats leaving the harbor through dawn mists. Artists were setting up easels. Suddenly, he knew: *Claire would love it here.*

That week, he bought a couch at one yard sale, and a table at another. When Claire's classes were done, they worked together to make a home of attic gleanings, paint, lumber, fabric—her art, his craft.

Summer came. So little time now! Claire's mother had prepared a layette and refinished a crib. Friends and family conspired to provide the rest, from car bed to washing machine.

All of us marveled at the events of these months. Wonders had been accomplished as if some benign power had been at work. Love! It was love—exactly that—which had come into focus again and again. This was the source of Chris's and Claire's faith, courage, and commitment, and of the caring involvement of friends and family. It had made the impossible possible.

Caitlin was born on a Sunday night in July. Her eyes opened wide as the light first fell on them; her fists pummeled the air. She let out a cry, announcing her arrival, and came into the world kicking.

The doctor delivered the baby, and gave her to Claire. Chris cut the cord. She was a rosy, pretty baby, perfect and strong—and *theirs*.

On Caitlin's christening day, the young parents and godparents assembled to accept their responsibilities toward her everlasting soul. She stretched out her arms like wings, her fingers like flight feathers. Then she lifted her still-wobbly head and smiled into every face she could see.

In her Maine grandmother's herb-hung kitchen, a feast was spread. The cake was piped with a single rose and the inscription: "God Bless Caitlin."

Only love can be divided

endlessly and still

not diminish.

ANNE MORROW LINDBERGH

A few days later, I visited the cottage. After supper, Caitlin turned colicky. I held her, soothing her to sleep. In the mute exhaustion of unslept new parents, Chris and Claire stretched out on the couch.

Caitlin's soft hair lay near my cheek. Just above my heart, her own was beating. One fist was curled in the hollow of my neck. The other had fallen on the air. Occasionally she startled in some infant dream. Her toes scrabbled for fresh purchase in my ribs, and she slept on. The weight of her, the heat of her, the breath of her felt inexpressibly exquisite to me.

Claire turned her head and tenderly studied her baby. "Are you tired?" she asked me.

"No," I said. "I'm happy."

Chris smiled. "I know," he said quietly. "It's a wonderful feeling."

Oh, my dear son, I thought, *you are everything your name implies.*

So goes the world around. Time in its season, grace in moments of true knowing. The children become the mothers and the fathers; and love begins again—at the beginning.

PROFESSOR TERRY AND THE LADY IN BROWN

BY

LOUIS NIZER

*P*rofessor Charles Thaddeus Terry taught "Contracts" at Columbia University Law School. He was about fifty-five when I was a student there. He had a clubfoot and walked with a limp. He was bald, and his face was so ferocious and ugly that there was almost beauty in its rugged asymmetry. His nose was both hooked and flattened, and it looked no better from supporting the pince-nez glasses on a black ribbon that shivered down to his vest. His mouth was thick-lipped and wide, and its glistening red inner skin showed when he talked.

As one might expect, no sweet voice could emanate from such a face. Instead, his deep baritone was constantly squeezed by sarcasm. And such sarcasm! He was a master at it. If he called out your name, it sounded as if you were an illegitimate child who had adopted a false name to disguise the bastardy.

He was unremittingly cruel. He humiliated. He taunted. He ridiculed. But how he taught! How he made you understand the majesty of the law and its philosophical striving for justice!

He used the Socratic teaching technique, asking questions, never giving answers. You had to find your own way, but he deliberately led you into byways so that you would learn your own way back and really understand the terrain. And no matter which way you answered, a barrage of questions threw doubt on your conclusion. He would begin with the most elementary lesson in contracts.

"Mr. Nizer, what is a contract?"

"It is a meeting of the minds, sir—an offer by one party which is accepted by another."

"Does the contract come into existence the moment the minds meet?"

"Yes, sir."

"Oh, it does, does it?" His snarl was like the sudden appearance of dark clouds preceding a storm. "Suppose A offers to sell his car for $3000 and sends his offer in writing to B. B writes his acceptance and puts it in the mail. Is that a contract?"

"Yes, sir. Because their minds have met on the deal."

"Even though A has not yet received B's letter of acceptance?"

Hesitantly, "Yes, sir."

"Suppose that A changes his mind and sends B a telegram withdrawing his offer, and the telegram is received by B before his letter of acceptance reaches A? Is there a contract?"

"Yes, sir. Their minds met on the offer when B mailed his acceptance."

Angrily, "But how can the offer which has been withdrawn by telegram be accepted? What is there to accept? Has not the offerer the right to withdraw his offer before the contract has been consummated?"

"Yes, sir."

"Then doesn't it follow that since A has withdrawn his offer, there is nothing to accept?"

"I can see that, sir."

"So you would change your previous answer, Mr. Nizer?" The name was pronounced so as to be synonymous with dunce.

"I believe I would. Yes, sir."

Professor Terry stared at me for a long time. Then he called on another student.

"Mr. Thomas, do you agree with Mr. Nizer's last answer?"

"Yes, Professor Terry."

"Why?"

"For the reason you gave, sir."

"I gave no reason. I asked questions. Stand on your own feet! I have asked you, 'Why?' "

"Well, because the offer was withdrawn by telegram, there was nothing to accept."

"Where do you get that idea from? If I hold out a proposal and you agree, haven't our minds met at the instant you accept? Besides, B's acceptance was not a mere mental concept. He wrote it out and placed it in a mailbox, beyond his power to control. Doesn't that make a difference?"

"Yes, sir, perhaps it would."

"*Perhaps?* It would, wouldn't it?" The booming voice exploded like a cannon shot, reverberating around the room.

"Yes, sir, it would."

Professor Terry gave Thomas a long stare, then turned to another student. "Mr. McGraw, with whom do you agree? With Mr. Nizer's *final* answer, or with Mr. Thomas's *final* answer?"

"I think there is a contract when B mails his letter of acceptance. Nothing thereafter can change that fact."

"Nothing can change that?" asked Professor Terry. The red glistened from his inner lower lip. "Suppose after B has mailed his letter of acceptance, he telephones A and says, 'I've decided not to buy your car. Ignore my letter, which you will receive.' Is there still a contract?"

"Yes, sir."

Professor Terry's face lighted up, announcing that the trap had been sprung. "Then suppose A sells his car to C. Can B sue for breach of contract?"

"Well . . ." McGraw, too, changed his mind.

It didn't matter what position the next student took. He was run down just as mercilessly. Eventually, it turned out that all of our answers were right. Some states follow one rule, some another; what would be held to be a contract in Massachusetts would not be in New York. So, even in the very first session, we learned that the law was not an exact science. It was a philosophical pursuit of moral precepts, and the logic used in the quest was not irrefutable.

Strangely enough, Professor Terry's uncompromising pressure, which often seemed tinged with viciousness, did not make us bitter toward him. In fact, a deep affection set in for the man. He encouraged our discussions with him after the lecture, as if he recognized that a runner who had run a hard race could not stop suddenly but must taper off. Crowded around him, we knew that the punishment he had meted out was for our own good. When, in the course of that more informal exchange at the podium, he put his hand on our shoulder, we felt as if we had been knighted.

Professor Terry became a legend at Columbia Law School. Thousands of students who passed through his classroom over the years remembered him above all other teachers. But our class was privileged to participate in a special event—an event that revealed a dimension no others had seen.

When Professor Terry announced his retirement, Dean Harlan F. Stone and the faculty decided to give him a farewell at which an oil painting of him would be hung in the library. Terry asked that the students be invited. We crowded into the library eagerly, but we had no inkling that what would happen would become perhaps the most moving experience of our young lives.

Seated on a raised tier with the professors was a lady all in brown. A beautiful young girl is an accident of nature, but a beautiful older woman is a work of art. She was a work of art, inexpressibly beautiful. Her perfectly proportioned features were enhanced by gentle, curving white hair, which added aristocracy rather than age to her face. Her neck was long, and she held her head regally high, but without a trace of hauteur. She sat motionless and attentive. We wondered who she was. All eyes were upon her, until the ceremonies and speeches drew attention away. When they concluded, with grace and not a little solemn dignity, Professor Terry rose to speak.

He stood motionless for a long time. We had never seen his face look as it did then. It had lost its severity. It looked pink and kind. The mouth was not a snarl. His voice, too, was different. It was soft, without a trace of belligerence or sarcasm.

After expressing gratitude for the painting, "which will keep fresh the memories of the torture I have imposed," he explained that he loved the law, and had the feeling that every student who had committed himself to the greatest of all professions was his son. Therefore, out of *love,* he had been remorseless in his training.

The mind can grow only if it is challenged, he said. Then, in self-defense, it calls upon its reserves of imagination and resourcefulness. The student must find his own way, as he will have to do in the outside world. That was why he was abrasive. The world outside would be *more* abrasive. He could not afford to be tolerant of anything but the best that was in us. He put into words the high purpose that had motivated most of us to enter the law, and he told us that his great satisfaction in

Love is a great beautifier.

LOUISA MAY ALCOTT

life was to see his students later become brilliant lawyers, judges, and public servants. He continued in this vein—an unaffected outpouring of idealism.

Then the unexpected happened. He took one of his long pauses, which had been so meaningful in the classroom. He turned toward the beautiful woman in brown:

"I have been expressing my gratitude to my students, my colleagues, and my school. But it is only a tiny portion of the gratitude which fills my heart. I cannot bid you all good-bye leaving unsaid that which is the most important thing in my life."

He looked down at his foot and continued, his voice hoarse with emotion. "At the age of thirty, I met the most beautiful girl I had ever seen. I was stunned and in love with her immediately. But I considered her unattainable for one such as I. Nature had not endowed me with any of the graces of appearance. I dared not even contemplate the audacity to confide my feelings to her. I was happy just to think of her, and this gratification I indulged in day and night.

"But she ordered events so as to bring us together. With delicacy and sensitivity, she told me that she knew how I felt about her, and that she was more in love with me than I could possibly be with her. I have been blinded by ecstasy ever since.

"Through the years that followed, we have reared a family in supreme happiness. She has dedicated her life and her love to me without reservation or pause even for the vicissitudes of life. Teaching, writing, and practicing law have been temporary absences made bearable only because I knew I was returning to her. Every thinking moment has had the silent musical accompaniment of her presence."

His voice grew hoarser as he struggled to eliminate the quiver that was entering it. "So, although it is farthest from my nature to discuss the most private of all emotions in public, I cannot in this leavetaking do other than tell you that I owe all my happiness to her, that she has . . ."

He turned his head toward her, and his eyes completed the sentence as if words could not possibly convey the depth of his feeling.

Tears were running down her cheeks, but she did not move. Her eyes were clear despite the streams, and she looked steadily at him. Their gazes met and locked in long silence. Then, without another word, he sat down.

No one applauded. We just sat there. After a few moments, everyone got up slowly and left.

Marriage should be a duet—when one

sings, the other claps.

JOE MURRAY

THE BEST KIND OF LOVE

BY

ANNETTE PAXMAN BOWEN

I have a friend who is falling in love. She honestly claims the sky is bluer. Mozart moves her to tears. She has lost 15 pounds and looks like a cover girl. "I'm young again!" she shouts exuberantly.

As my friend raves on about her new love, I've taken a good look at my old one. My husband of almost 20 years, Scott, has gained 15 pounds. Once a marathon runner, he now runs only down hospital halls. His hairline is receding, and his body shows the signs of long work hours and too many candy bars. Yet he can still give me a certain look across a restaurant table and I want to ask for the check and head home.

When my friend asked me "What will make this love last?" I ran through all the obvious reasons: commitment, shared interests, unselfishness, physical attraction, communication. Yet there's more.

We still have fun. Spontaneous good times. Once, after slipping the rubber band off the rolled-up newspaper, Scott flipped it playfully at me: this led to an all-out war. Another time, at the grocery, we split the list and raced each other to see who could make it to the checkout first. Even washing dishes can be a blast. We enjoy simply being together.

And there are surprises. One time I came home to find a note on the front door that led me to another note, then another, until I reached the walk-in closet. I opened the door to find Scott holding a "pot of gold" (my cooking kettle) and the "treasure" of a gift package. Sometimes I leave him notes on the mirror and little presents under his pillow.

There is understanding. I understand why he must play basketball with the guys. And he understands why, once a year, I must get away from the house, the kids—and even him—to meet my sisters for a few days of nonstop talking and laughing.

There is sharing. Not only do we share household worries and parental burdens—we also share ideas. Scott came home from a convention once and presented me with a thick historical novel. Though he prefers thrillers and science fiction, he had read the novel on the plane. He touched my heart when he explained it was because he wanted to be able to exchange ideas about the book after I'd read it.

There is forgiveness. When I'm embarrassingly loud and crazy at parties, Scott forgives me. When he confessed losing some of our savings in the stock market, I gave him a hug and said, "It's okay. It's only money."

There is sensitivity. One evening he walked through the door with that look that tells me it's been a tough day. After he spent some time with the kids, I asked him what happened. He told me about a sixty-year-old woman who'd had a stroke. He wept as he recalled the woman's husband standing beside her bed, caressing her hand. How was he going to tell this husband of 40 years that his wife would probably never recover?

I shed a few tears myself. Because of the medical crisis. Because there were still people who have been married 40 years. Because my husband is still moved and concerned after years of hospital rooms and dying patients.

There is faith. One day a friend came over and confessed her fear that her husband is losing his courageous battle with cancer. The following afternoon I went to lunch with a friend who is struggling to reshape her life after divorce. The next day a neighbor called to talk about the frightening effects of Alzheimer's disease on her father-in-law's personality. Then a childhood friend called long-distance to tell me her father had died. I hung up the phone and thought, *This is too much heartache for one week.*

After saying a prayer, I descended the stairs to run some errands. Through my tears, I noticed the boisterous orange blossoms of the gladiolus outside my window. I heard the delighted laughter of my son and his friend as they played in our basement. After backing out of my driveway, I caught sight of a wedding party emerging from a neighbor's house. The bride, dressed in satin and lace, tossed her bouquet to her cheering friends.

That night I told my husband about these events. We helped each other acknowledge the cycles of life and that joys counter the sorrows. It was enough to keep us going.

Finally, there is knowing. I know Scott will throw his laundry just shy of the hamper every night; he'll be late to most appointments and eat the last chocolate in the box. He knows I sleep with a pillow over my head; I'll lock us out of the house on a regular basis, and I will also eat the last chocolate.

I guess our love lasts because it's comfortable. No, the sky is not bluer: it's just a familiar hue. We don't feel particularly young: we've experienced too much that's contributed to growth and wisdom, taken its toll on our bodies, and created our memories.

I hope we've got what it takes to make our love last. As a bride, I had Scott's wedding band engraved with Robert Browning's line "Grow old along with me!" We're following those instructions.

A good marriage is like an incredible retirement
fund. You put everything you have into it during
your productive life, and over the years it turns
from silver to gold to platinum.

WILLARD SCOTT

THE DREAM HORSE AND THE DINING-ROOM TABLE

BY

BILLY PORTERFIELD

Since he was a kid on the Oklahoma prairie, Daddy loved the sweet, nutty smell of horses and mules. He had grown up working them in the fields. On Saturday afternoons, he had raced horses in country fairs. He liked being in the saddle so much that he used his for a pillow in bed. It took some doing for Mother to get used to that.

If horses were Daddy's passion, working on oil rigs was his job. He was an experienced roughneck on a drilling crew. The money was good while the rig was running. But when a well was finished, the drilling crew had to move on. So our family drifted from job to job through the oil fields of Oklahoma and East Texas.

Daddy staggered drilling work with roustabouting: looking after existing wells and tank farms. The hourly wage was lower than on a rig, but the work was steady, the check came every week, and the company provided a house. These were never fancy, but our family made them home, however short our stay.

It was at one of these lease houses in Texas that Daddy bought War Cloud—a white-eyed, dapple-gray stallion. War Cloud was Daddy's dream horse. Every dawn before work, he spent an hour in the stable, feeding the stallion crimped oats and brushing his coat. Evenings, he rode until sunset.

He outfitted War Cloud's stall with every amenity: running water, a salt block, a tack box, blankets for every kind of weather, and a cabinet with all the ointments and pills an ailing horse could need. There was even a fan to keep the flies off.

Mother claimed the stable was furnished better than our company house. She tried to pretty things up for us, making oval throw rugs for the living room and bedrooms. Our floors were so clean you could eat off them. But she still wasn't satisfied. We ate at a table a neighbor gave us. It was rough and unpainted and she kept it hidden under oilcloth. Mother wanted a *real* dining-room suite.

One day she spotted a varnished walnut table and six chairs in the nearby town of Benavides. She could see it at home, covered with a lacy white tablecloth. But the set cost $100. At that price Daddy wouldn't even look at it. *Had the woman lost her mind?*

So our tiny mother put her dream aside and went on with her days—kneeling down, scrubbing the linoleum, standing out back at the roller washing machine, or bending over the ironing board, pressing jeans with a heavy steam iron. She smelled of soap and scorched cotton. We used to say Daddy wore the only starched, ironed underwear in the oil patch.

Mother had such a passion for spit and polish and the rightness of work that she was in perpetual motion. But all along, we sensed she was strangely fragile. In the fall of the year Daddy bought War Cloud, she finally pushed her body beyond endurance and came down sick. She ran a fever, had chills, and vomited all over the place.

An old Mexican doctor came out from Benavides, bent over the bed, and realized that Mother, already run-down and anemic, had eaten something spoiled. "She has ptomaine poisoning," he said. "It'll be touch and go because her fever is so high and she's terribly dehydrated."

47

Mother lapsed into a coma. We thought she was going to die. She came out of it, but then she kissed us all and settled into a strange calm.

Fay Talbot, a neighbor, moved in to keep Mother full of aspirin and liquids. Every morning she bathed her in bed and changed her gown and sheets. Each day, the doc drove the 15 miles from Benavides. He said there was nothing to do but wait and pray.

Daddy slept on the living-room divan. One morning, he went out to the stable, where he thought we couldn't see him, and bawled. This rough man babbled to God, promising anything if his wife would get well. "I'll sell War Cloud, I'll buy that new dining-room suite, if only you'll bring her around."

We were never quite sure if it was Daddy's prayer, the old doctor's medicine, Fay Talbot's nursing, or her own drive, but Mother did recover. The day she thought she'd get out of bed and try her legs, Daddy slipped out and hauled War Cloud to the stock auctioneer in Benavides. He sold his pride to the highest bidder for $150.

Why he then went out and got drunk has always been a matter of family debate. I lean to the side that has him drowning in self-pity for losing his head and making such a promise to God. When it came down to death's door, he chose his wife over his horse. But now death had been set back, and his wife was on the mend. He might have figured he could have got by without losing either.

Anyway, after stupefying himself, my father staggered to the furniture store and bought the dining-room suite and a lacy white tablecloth. When he got back to the house, we kids—laughing and whispering—helped him set it up. Then we helped Mother out of bed and walked her to the dining room for the surprise.

"Well," Daddy asked, "what do you think?"

Mother's heart rose. Daddy had done a wonderful thing.

Then her heart fell: *It was the wrong suite.* This tacky furniture was not walnut, it was plain oak, painted blond.

She looked at her husband. She looked at her children. Tears came into her eyes.

"Why, Daddy—my darlings," she said, leaning on her husband, "it's perfectly beautiful. I love it."

Mother used that suite for 37 years, moving it wherever we went. One day, she stripped the painted finish and discovered a lovely natural grain in the wood. Then she stained it the deep walnut she'd always wanted. After Mother died, my sister took the table for her dining room.

We knew Mother was right. Painted or not, Daddy's table was perfectly beautiful.

Come live with me and be my love,
And we will some new pleasures prove
Of golden sands, and crystal brooks,
With silken lines, and silver hooks.

JOHN DONNE

"YOU WILL HAVE A GOOD LIFE"

BY

KATHARINE BYRNE

Alone now much of the time, the widow reads a lot. She used to underline favorite passages to share with her husband. Now, the quotations are stored in a notebook. These lines from Elizabeth Jolley's *Cabin Fever*, for example: "I experience again the deep-felt wish to be part of a married couple, to sit by the fire in winter with the man who is my husband. So intense is this wish that if I write the word *husband* on a piece of paper, my eyes fill with tears."

Why are these lines so painful?

We can start with a worn wedding album. In the first picture, the bride and groom are facing, with uncertain smiles, a church filled with relatives and friends. The bride did not wear glasses that day, so everything was a blur of candlelight, poinsettias, and faces.

They walked to the back of the church and stood at the door as their guests filed past. From colleagues and old schoolmates came cheerful expressions of good will clothed in clumsy jokes. Some relatives, however, were not pleased. One sat in a car, sobbing. Another stood surrounded by sympathizers offering condolences. Both these women—mothers of the bride and groom—would have insisted they wanted only the best for their children. But "the best" they defined as staying home to help support the family.

The last person to approach the couple was a short, sturdy woman who smiled as she congratulated them—not by name but as "wife" and "husband."

"I'm Aunt Esther Gubbins," she said. "I'm here to tell you that you are going to live a good life and be happy. You will work hard and love each other."

Then quickly, for such a stout and elderly person, she was gone.

Soon they were off, in a borrowed car. With money lent by the groom's brother, they could afford a few days at a state-park lodge. Sitting before a great oak fire, they reviewed the events of the day, remembering the good wishes of their friends, the anguish of their mothers, and the strange message conveyed by Aunt Esther Gubbins.

"Is she your mother's sister or your father's?" asked the wife.

"Isn't she *your* aunt?" the husband replied. "I never saw her before."

They wondered. Had she come to the wrong church or at the wrong time, mistaking them for another couple? Or was she just an old woman who liked weddings and looked for announcements in church bulletins?

With the passage of time and the accumulation of grandchildren, their mothers became reconciled to the marriage. One made piles of play clothes for the children; the other crocheted and knitted bonnets, mittens, sweaters, and scarves.

The couple's life together was unremarkable. Oddly, neither ever asked "Whose job is this?" or asserted "That is not my responsibility!" Both acted to fill needs as time and opportunity allowed: groping in the

medicine chest for eardrops in the middle of the night to soothe a crying child; tossing in one more load of whites from the perpetual pile at the base of the clothes chute.

Arriving from work, he might stand at the door and announce, "Wife, I am home!" And she, restraining the impulse to let loose a string of well-founded complaints, would call from some corner of the house, "Husband, I am glad!"

Once in a while, usually around their anniversary, they would dredge up the old curiosity regarding Aunt Esther Gubbins. He would insist that the elderly woman had been present at their wedding only accidentally. But she knew that Aunt Esther was on some heavenly mission. At such times, even their children took sides: the earthbound against the fantasists.

Now, alone, the wife asks herself what she would save from the old house if it were to catch fire. Her mother's cameo? Pictures of her husband? The vault key? The $47 hidden in the sugar bowl?

No, it would be the frayed, yellowing envelope she has kept for so long. A woman who spends a lot of time looking for things, she knows exactly where it can be found: under a pile of Madeira napkins used on celebratory occasions.

The husband had fallen asleep in his chair one evening, nodding over a spy novel. She wrote a note on the back of the envelope and left it on his book: "Husband, I have gone next door to help Mrs. Norton figure out her Medicare reimbursements."

The next morning she saw that he had written below her message: "Wife, I missed you. You thought I was asleep, but I was just resting my eyes and thinking about that woman who talked to us in church a long time ago. It has always seemed to me that she was the wrong shape for a heavenly messenger. Anyway, it's time to stop wondering whether she came from heaven or the next parish. What matters is this: whoever she was, Aunt Esther Gubbins was right."

To love and be loved is to feel the sun from

both sides.

DAVID VISCOTT

A LOVE LIKE NO OTHER

BY

SKIP HOLLANDSWORTH

From the day she was born, doctors had expected Kimberley Marshall to die. She had cystic fibrosis, a baffling genetic disorder. Desperate to keep her baby alive, Kim's mother, Dawn, took the infant home and for three hours a day she and Kim's grandmother gently thumped on her chest and back to dislodge the sticky mucus that clogs the lungs of CF patients. Trying to get rid of it, one doctor says, is like sweeping spilled molasses off the floor with a broom.

To everyone's astonishment, Kim eventually grew strong enough to go to elementary school. She even took ballet lessons and joined a girls' soccer team.

"There goes the princess," Dawn would shout from the sidelines, momentarily allowing herself to feel as normal as the other mothers. She imagined Kim to be normal, too, the kind of girl who might go to a high-school dance and lift her head dreamily at the end of the night, as a boy gave her her first kiss.

But Robert Kramer, the first doctor in Dallas to specialize in CF, warned Dawn and her husband, Bill, that it was only a temporary

56

reprieve. Like a serial killer, CF is unstoppable. Although an array of pulmonary treatments and medicines now allows patients to live more productive, pain-free lives, average life expectancy is about 29 years.

As Doctor Kramer predicted, the days soon came when Kim's body seemed to deflate like a rubber toy with a hole in it, and Dawn would return her to the Presbyterian Hospital of Dallas. The routine became all too familiar: a few months of remission followed by a trip to the hospital's CF unit.

Kim always brought along her stuffed animals, her favorite pink blanket, and her diary. As children around her died, she'd write down her impressions ("Wendy died at 8:10 this morning! She suffered all night. It's better this way. Poor little thing"). It was, Dawn thought, Kim's way of preparing herself for what she knew would someday happen to her.

For a while Kim did what she could to be like the "normals" (her nickname for kids without CF). In high school she earned A's and B's and wore long dresses to hide her spindly legs. When classmates asked about her coughing spells, she would say she suffered from asthma. She'd pick up other CF girls in her car and drive along, honking her horn, waving at boys and flashing a jubilant smile.

Still, she could not ignore the reality of her life. Her digestive system was so clogged with mucus that she suffered painful attacks of diarrhea. She developed a neurological disorder that affected her balance and distorted her perception.

Finally, during her senior year, she grew so weak that she had to finish her course work at home. In one of her lowest moments she asked that her picture not be included in her high-school yearbook. "I look like a starvation victim," she said. Growing increasingly frustrated, Kim argued often with her younger brother and sister. Over and over she watched a videotape of *The Blue Lagoon,* the story of an adolescent boy and girl who are stranded on an island and fall in love.

David Crenshaw first laid eyes on Kim in the spring of 1986 when both were being treated at Presbyterian. She was sixteen, thin, pale, and beautiful, her red hair falling down the back of her pink nightgown. David was eighteen. He wore a baggy T-shirt, faded gray pajama pants, and large glasses held together by a piece of tape.

"No way she's going to look twice at you," teased Doug Kellum, one of the CF unit's respiratory therapists, who had noticed David staring at her. And, indeed, it was difficult to imagine any attraction between them. Kim loved expensive perfume, makeup, and clothes. She would sit for hours in her hospital bed, reading romance novels.

David, on the other hand, was famous for trying to impress girls with crude jokes. Loud and robust, he was something of a legend at Presbyterian. No one had ever heard of a CF patient doing the things David did. For instance, when he wasn't in the hospital, he raced midget cars at a local dirt track. "Our goal was to raise him as if he weren't sick," says David's father. "Maybe I thought if he stayed tough enough, he could beat it."

In truth, David never did act particularly sick. A prankster, he conducted wheelchair races and tomato-throwing competitions in the hospital's third-floor hallway. One night he took some CF patients to a go-cart track in 32-degree weather. "He had this sense of immortality about him," Doctor Kramer remembers.

For two years David would often walk past Kim's door, working up the courage to pop in and say hello. Kim would look at him, smile briefly, then go back to reading her book.

David was undaunted. "When she was in the hospital and he was home," Kellum says, "he'd call me to find out how she was—even though she wouldn't give him the time of day."

Surprisingly, it is often in the CF unit that young patients experience their first encounter with romance. "You assume that because CF kids look so weak, they don't have much of a sex drive," says Doctor Kramer.

"Yet they probably think about it more than regular people. It's their way of affirming to themselves that they are alive and kicking."

In late 1988 Kim began an on-again, off-again relationship with another CF patient, a young man named Steve. "I knew it wasn't going to work out," David said. "They were afraid of commitment." And the relationship did finally falter.

In the fall of 1989, when he and Kim were both at home once again, David called and asked her to dinner. Although she said no, David declared, "I'll be there at 8:00 P.M., no buts about it."

Horrified, Kim brought along her sister, Petri, and made her sit with David in the front seat of his car while she sat in the back, refusing to speak. Kim also remained silent through dinner, and gave David a tortured look when he suggested they go dancing at a nightclub. When he took her home, Kim leapt out of the car and ran to her room.

Still, David kept showing up at Kim's house. They went bowling. He took her to watch him race. And, despite everything, love bloomed. On November 17, 1989, Kim wrote in her diary: "Tonight, David and I kissed for the first time. God, please let this relationship work out."

Six months after their first date, Kim and David announced their engagement—to the shock of their families, friends, and doctors. "Both of you are sick," David's father said, pleading with him to reconsider. "You can't possibly take care of yourselves." "Do you realize that one of you is going to die in the other's arms?" Dawn asked her daughter tearfully.

Kim and David insisted that they had a right to be together. "I think Kim realized this was going to be the last chance she had to experience love," Dawn said, finally agreeing to the union.

On October 27, 1990, Kim Marshall, twenty-one, wobbled down the aisle and declared her love for twenty-three-year-old David Crenshaw. The church was filled with the sound of coughing, as Dallas's CF community came to support them.

The couple lived on their modest monthly disability checks in a one-bedroom apartment. It resembled a hospital room, crammed with oxygen tanks, medicines, and a refrigerator stocked with I.V. bottles.

Domestic tasks were difficult: They needed a day to clean the apartment and do the laundry. By nighttime both were exhausted. Yet they were happier than they ever could have imagined. He nicknamed her Tigger (from the children's book *Winnie the Pooh*) because of her red hair; she called him Bear because he was cuddly. He was always sending her cards, the mushier the better. She wrote him long love letters. ("We are going to conquer the unconquerable.")

To earn extra income, David worked rebuilding race cars. He also enrolled at a junior college to get an accounting degree. One of his CF friends, Richard Johnson, warned him it was impossible to keep up such a pace. David just said, "I've got to do this for Kim. There isn't anything in my life but her."

By 1992 Kim's veins had begun to collapse. Because her body was unable to absorb food through her clogged digestive system, she was rapidly losing weight. She became ashamed to show herself in public. "Tigger," David wrote her, "you are the most beautiful woman I know inside and out. I love you with all my heart and soul! Bear."

David never left Kim's side during her frequent trips to the hospital. He would sleep on a cot in her room. To entertain her, he wheeled her to the maternity ward so she could look at the babies. If she wanted candy

Marrying for love may be a bit risky, but it is so honest that God can't help but smile on it.

JOSH BILLINGS

in the middle of the night, he'd go out and buy her some. Amazingly, Kim's health improved, and she returned home.

Then, in early 1993, David's condition worsened. His cough grew louder and deeper. His face got puffy from fluid retention. Eventually he, too, breathed with the assistance of a portable oxygen machine.

David assured Kim there was nothing to worry about; he just had to build up his strength. He didn't tell her what Doctor Kramer had said after a recent checkup: David's lungs were becoming stiff with scar tissue and his bronchial tubes were closing up. He was slowly choking to death.

It was a race against time, and David would not waste a single moment. In July, to celebrate his twenty-sixth birthday and Kim's twenty-fourth, he insisted they take a weeklong Florida vacation. "Only once did they feel good enough to leave the condo and go to the beach," says Kim's sister, Mandy, who traveled with them. "Both carried their portable oxygen tanks. They sat on the beach holding hands."

Three months later, David and Kim went for a checkup. While Kim waited in another room, Doctor Kramer studied David's oxygen levels. "You've got to go into the hospital," he said. "And this time, you may be there for a long time." David managed only one response: "Make sure Kim is okay."

Kramer walked across the hall to tell her. Kim dropped her head and tried not to cry. "Don't let him suffer, Doctor Bob," she said. During his 30 years as a CF specialist, Kramer had watched more than 400 young patients die. For his own sanity, he distanced himself emotionally from cases like David's. But now he gathered Kim in his arms and wept.

David was admitted to the hospital on October 21. Kim sat by his side. She tried to write a letter to Medicare officials, begging them to consider him for a lung transplant, a last resort for a few CF patients, but she never got to finish it. Five days later, David's lips and fingernails turned blue.

"David, not yet," she said. Unable to speak, he mouthed "I love you" and blew her a kiss. Kim and David exchanged one long look of grief and love. Moments later he died.

Within 24 hours of his funeral, Kim went into a state of shock. A week later Dawn took her to the hospital. After seeing her, Doctor Kramer offered a decidedly unmedical diagnosis to her parents. "Her body is giving up," he told them. "It's as if she were dying of a broken heart."

Kim was semicomatose for two days. Then, early on the morning of November 11, she regained consciousness, opened her eyes, and began speaking in a peaceful, cooing voice that no one could understand. A nurse said it sounded as if she were talking to David. Then she shut her eyes and died.

Kim was buried in her wedding dress alongside her husband. Their tombstone reads: "David S. (Bear) Crenshaw and Kimberley (Tigger) Crenshaw . . . Together forever. Married three years."

All their friends and family agreed theirs had been a love story like no other. "To me," said Doctor Kramer, "it was Romeo and Juliet all over again."

Weeks later, Dawn was sorting through the couple's possessions. She came across the last card David had sent Kim before he died. "We are close even when we are apart," it read. "Just look up. We are both under the same starry sky."

For a crowd is not company; and faces are

but a gallery of pictures; and talk but a

tinkling cymbal, where there is no love.

FRANCIS BACON

MY FAVORITE VALENTINE

BY
CHUCK THOMPSON

For me there has been only one Valentine's Day worthy of the name. Fourth grade. A girl named Lori. No Valentine's Day since has even come close to measuring up.

Her image has never left my mind, and on a recent Valentine's Day the idea got stuck in my head: I needed to find Lori.

1972. Southern California. For two years I have been in love with Lori, an angelic creature who lives across the street. Our walk home from the bus stop each day is the highlight of my young life.

The situation is complicated. First, Lori's older brother, Ted, happens to be my best friend. Second, I am grotesquely bashful in Lori's presence. In the company of friends I am a sparkling wit. With Lori I communicate chiefly in grunts. Although she is always sweet to me, Lori's heart does not appear to pound to the same desperate rhythm as my own.

The whole thing comes to a head on Valentine's Day. In class, kids pass out store-bought cards, and I get a generic "Be Mine!" from Lori and the other 26 students.

On the walk home from the bus stop that day, however, Lori says, "I have something for you." I go numb. She pulls an oversized red envelope from her school bag, presses it into my hand, and takes off running.

I rush to my bedroom, carefully open the envelope, and find the most beautiful handmade card of red construction paper, and a big white doily, shiny stars, and all sorts of hearts. Inside, Lori has spelled out "I love you" in white glue and covered the perfect cursive letters with glitter. After reading it 30 or 40 times, I hide the card under my socks.

Lori and I might be married now for all I know—if not for one extenuating factor: my older brother, Mike. Pawing through my dresser that evening, he stumbled upon the envelope.

Now Mike was a sixth-grader, given to the sort of cruelty that earns big brothers bad reputations. He showed Lori's card to Ted and some other kids in the neighborhood. The commotion that ensued mortified Lori and me, and pretty much crushed any major developments in this early love.

Then my father announced that we would be moving to, of all places, Alaska. It seemed a rather severe place to be exiled from the summery smile of Lori. I suggested that I stay behind and live in an orphanage. But in the end there was little I could do.

At school Miss Lockhart organized a good-bye party. All I could do was stare at Lori—who, for the first time since Valentine's Day, stared back at me with great liquid eyes.

On the bus Lori sat next to me and clasped my hand the entire way home. At my door I searched for words to describe the terrific bursting in my chest.

"Well," I finally managed, " 'bye."

Lori kissed me on the cheek and darted across the street. Just like that, she was gone.

It had crossed my mind more than once that a search for a fourth-grade sweetheart does not indicate an entirely level mind. But where

there had once been romance, I had faith that some feeling remained. I was determined to travel to wherever the winds of fate had taken her, and then . . . who knows?

Phone calls to the old school and past acquaintances turned up nothing. Then a lawyer suggested a company that locates hard-to-find individuals. Within an hour of my call, the company had tracked Lori.

Until then, my pursuit had been half based on whimsical fantasy, but the address was a frighteningly real piece of information. *Do I really want to do this? Is it worth risking one of my most sacrosanct memories for disappointment?* But it would be stupid to finally get this close to Lori and then stand on the precipice, forever wondering.

"Dear Lori," my letter began, "I hope you haven't forgotten me." An entire afternoon was spent on that letter. I mailed it for overnight delivery.

The phone rang the next evening. "Of course I remember!" the voice began.

"Lori?"

"You had a dog named Walter."

"Yeah."

"You wore an Oakland Raiders jacket to school every day, even when it was too warm for a jacket."

"Yeah."

"You slugged a kid at the bus stop once for making fun of me when I had the chicken pox."

"Lori."

"Hey, stranger!"

We talked for an hour and laughed about what jerks our brothers were to us. Somewhere in the conversation she got around to her job and her husband and her two sons. I reviewed the high points of my life, and she seemed genuinely interested. She agreed to meet me at a restaurant the following week.

"You are Mr. Thompson?" asks the waiter at the restaurant. I nod. "A message from Lori. With regret she will be one hour late."

Lori's tardiness comes as something of a reprieve. My stomach has been in knots all day, and it might be good to have a few moments to collect myself.

Outside, I walk around the block, inventing a hundred explanations for Lori's delay: She had to work late. Could not find a sitter. A row with her husband, an insane rage-a-holic who has vowed to crush my spleen.

At once I am overtaken with a great epiphany: I don't need to go through with this to satisfy my curiosity about what might have been. I've known all along what I needed to know about Lori.

Nobody wants to find that two decades have muddied whatever connection there once might have been, not made it more heroic. That may be what life is all about, but it's not what fourth-grade love affairs are about.

Not far from the restaurant, I find a stationery store and buy paper, envelopes, white glue, and glitter. Sitting on a stoop, I write:

Lori,

I'm sure we would have had a wonderful time tonight, but all I really wanted to do was say thanks for that Valentine card you gave me a long time ago. It may feel like a small gesture to you, but those are the gifts that sum up everything that is good in the world. I will never forget you for it.

Yours, Chuck

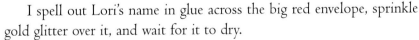

I spell out Lori's name in glue across the big red envelope, sprinkle gold glitter over it, and wait for it to dry.

Back at the restaurant, I seal the envelope with the most innocent kiss I can manage, place the card on our table, and walk quietly out the door.

WEDDING TALES

BY

ROBERT FULGHUM

When the excited voice on the telephone asks, "Mr. Fulghum, will you marry me?" I almost always accept. It's something I have been doing for nearly 30 years as an ordained minister. But my wife still looks up with a start when she hears me say, "Yes, of course I'll marry you."

Sometimes explosive, often hilarious, always enlightening, weddings are rarely dull. And a good deal of what we need to know about marriage is often revealed right there during the ceremony.

A Unitarian minister is often asked to perform interfaith or "mixed" marriages. Joining two people in such a marriage is like trying to cross a minefield without getting blown apart.

The paradigm of this kind of wedding involved a lovely young woman from Brooklyn. Huge family. Polish immigrant stock. Jewish. Her tall, dark, and handsome fiancé hailed from Detroit. Huge family. Irish immigrant stock. And Catholic. The bride's family included a rabbi and a cantor; the other team boasted some priests and a nun.

Ms. Brooklyn and Mr. Detroit were twenty-one years old and quite certain that love could find a way through any obstacle.

When the couple called their parents with the news, the mothers were united in their response. "YOU'RE MARRYING A WHAT?" followed by sobbing.

For a month the mail and phone calls flowed as uncles and aunts joined the fray. The families were NOT COMING, EVER, to such a wedding.

No matter; nothing could dissuade the couple. They came from tough, resilient folks who had always told their kids not to back off when they believed in something. The kids believed in each other.

Not that the bride and groom were unmoved. They spent a lot of time in my office—the bride bawled, the groom swore. But the marriage was meant to be, for the couple had an invisible shield: Love. And secret weapons: a sense of humor, light hearts. They laughed as often as they cried.

The tiebreaker in this standoff was the groom's grandmother. By heaven, if her only grandson was getting married, she was going to be there. Period. Grandma bought a plane ticket.

Thus the dominoes fell. Grandmother would need support. So, pretty soon all the Irish Catholics from Detroit were coming. Well, you know what happened next. Thirty-five Brooklyn Jews had plane tickets.

The wedding began to shape up like a grudge match between Notre Dame and Jerusalem Tech. Grandfather Rabbi begged to say a traditional blessing in Hebrew at the end of the service. When the Irish got wind of this, nothing would do but to have the grandmother sing "Ave Maria" before the blessing.

Come the great day, the families marched into the church and sat down on either side of the aisle. I would have given six-to-five odds in favor of a free-for-all following the ceremony.

Ah, but I keep forgetting Love: the Irish from Detroit loved the groom, no less than Brooklyn loved the bride. And when the couple said their vows, it was clear they meant every word. The bride began to weep, and the groom took her in his arms and wept too—well, the whole thing ground to a halt while everybody had a good cry, myself included. Joy, and a wordless affirmation, took us all by surprise.

Then the seventy-eight-year-old grandmother of the groom rose to sing "Ave Maria." Never have I heard it offered with more feeling, passion, and fervor.

Brooklyn gave her a standing ovation. They knew music and great love when they saw it. Grandmother was their kind of guy.

Not about to be outdone, Grandfather Rabbi took the bride's and groom's hands in his and laid a blessing on the couple to last them the rest of their lives. So, of course, the Irish gave Grandfather Rabbi a standing ovation.

After the ceremony the bride and groom rushed to the reception hall. The newlyweds danced, and everyone applauded. Never had I seen such a reception, such dancing, laughing, and singing, long into the night.

In the end, the bride and groom were right. Love *is* more powerful than prejudice. This wedding made me a believer.

Remember Goldilocks? She wanted everything to be "just right," as you may recall, and ended up in a bed belonging to an angry bear.

My next story is about a couple determined to have the Perfect Wedding—and have it outdoors to boot. They marched through details of the event like generals planning a siege.

Nothing could go wrong. It was a *big* wedding—400 people, black tie, summer hats, more attendants than a queen has. Truth to tell, they actually *had* a Perfect Wedding—until the bottom of the ninth inning.

The ceremony went fine. Boring—but smooth. I pronounced the couple husband and wife, and they turned to the smiling guests before striding down the grassy aisle to live happily ever after.

Meanwhile.

The bride's Uncle Harry had decided that a small fireworks display would be the Perfect Ending to this Perfect Wedding. So he had nailed rockets and Roman candles to a two-by-four and placed the board a short distance from the guests. As the bride and groom stood poised to walk back down the aisle, Uncle Harry lit the fuse. But when he turned to run away, he tripped—and kicked over the board. The one with the lit fireworks on it.

Uncle Harry just had time to scream "WATCH OUT!" before the first salvo was fired in the direction of the crowd. The Charge of the Light Brigade was nothing compared with the exodus of those assembled. I had seen many brides and grooms recess, but never a couple run for their lives.

Fortunately, the rockets went just high enough to pass about two feet overhead, so nobody was hit. A few of the slow-footed got bowled over in the melee, and several ladies ran headlong into blackberry bushes, but none of them got more than their dignity bruised.

Fortunately, the video cameraman didn't miss a thing. The tape was played again and again to the delight of the guests, who by now had loosened up and agreed that the footage of the stampede was the highlight of the day. People talked about that wedding for years.

It wasn't a Perfect Wedding, but it was a Great One—there were flaws, unexpected difficulties, and a little confusion, just like life itself.

The truth is that perfect marriages don't exist any more than perfect weddings. When couples accept this, they are freed to work toward true greatness—not in detail, but in spirit and passion and Love.

HOW LOVE CAME BACK

BY

TOM ANDERSON

I made a vow to myself on the drive down to the vacation beach cottage. For two weeks I would try to be a loving husband and father. Totally loving. No ifs, ands, or buts.

The idea had come to me as I listened to a commentator on my car's tape player. He was quoting a Biblical passage about husbands being thoughtful of their wives. Then he went on to say, "Love is an act of will. A person can *choose* to love." To myself, I had to admit that I had been a selfish husband—that our love had been dulled by my own insensitivity. In petty ways, really: chiding Evelyn for her tardiness; insisting on the TV channel *I* wanted to watch; throwing out day-old newspapers that I knew Evelyn still wanted to read. Well, for two weeks all that would change.

And it did. Right from the moment I kissed Evelyn at the door and said, "That new yellow sweater looks great on you."

"Oh, Tom, you noticed," she said, surprised and pleased. Maybe a little perplexed.

After the long drive, I wanted to sit and read. Evelyn suggested a walk on the beach. I started to refuse, but then I thought, *Evelyn's been alone here with the kids all week and now she wants to be alone with me.* We walked on the beach while the children flew their kites.

So it went. Two weeks of not calling the Wall Street investment firm where I am a director; a visit to the shell museum, though I usually hate museums (and I enjoyed it); holding my tongue while Evelyn's getting ready made us late for a dinner date. Relaxed and happy, that's how the whole vacation passed. I made a new vow to keep on remembering to *choose* love.

There was one thing that went wrong with my experiment, however. Evelyn and I still laugh about it today. On the last night at our cottage, preparing for bed, Evelyn stared at me with the saddest expression.

"What's the matter?" I asked her.

"Tom," she said, in a voice filled with distress, "do you know something I don't?"

"What do you mean?"

"Well . . . that checkup I had several weeks ago . . . our doctor . . . did he tell you something about me? Tom, you've been so good to me . . . am I dying?"

It took a moment for it all to sink in. Then I burst out laughing.

"No, honey," I said, wrapping her in my arms, "you're not dying; I'm just starting to live!"

LOVE STORY

BY

COLLIN PERRY

He was going to be gone for six months. *That's not so bad*, Kim thought as she packed his suitcase. *A relationship needs time—we just met a year ago. This will give us a chance to sort things out. So why am I so upset? Sure, six months, but in a Godforsaken place like Somalia!*

"It's simple, Kim," Ken had said during one of their discussions on his decision to leave their hometown of Boulder, Colorado, to work as a loan officer in the war-ravaged African country. "That's where I'm needed."

"But these people are *killing* Americans. They don't want our help!"

"The warlords don't want us there, but the guy who needs a loan to buy cattle so he can feed his family does."

"Okay, then what about me, Ken? *I* need you too."

He flashed his boyish, disarming smile. "And I need you, Kim. I'll be back before you know it."

"Aren't you afraid?" she asked as they embraced.

"Afraid? Me?" He looked at her, his hazel eyes twinkling. "Nah."

That's one of the things that had attracted Kim Schwers, twenty-six, to Ken Rutherford, thirty—those vibrant eyes. On their first date she had sensed something in the handsome, six-foot-one former football player beyond the charm and social ease. In his eyes, she saw something radiant.

Kim was surprised at how many people knew Ken—especially people eager to thank him for something. He was always volunteering for a charity drive or helping out a friend.

Kim's business experience as a consultant for a management-training firm had taught her always to look for the catch. But the deeper she scratched the surface, the more generosity, warmth, and integrity she found in Ken Rutherford. Soon she was hooked. And Ken was equally taken with this pretty, athletic, sandy-haired woman with the prickly wit.

Okay, I can't pretend to understand, she thought, slamming his suitcase shut. *But he'll be back, and we'll be together. So why am I angry?*

Their good-bye at the airport was difficult—but tender. "I love you, Ken," whispered Kim.

"I love you too," he replied gently. Then he turned and disappeared down the ramp. It was August 8, 1993.

"All right, Abdullah, how many applicants today?" Ken asked one of his Somali aides on the morning of December 16. Ken glanced out the credit-union window at the noisy gathering of primitive carts, braying mules, and turbaned Somalis on the main street of Luuq. The carts were used to transport water-filled drums to households and small businesses.

"We have eighty applicants scheduled."

"Eighty?" said Ken, sighing. "In a town of no more than fifty carts." He knew owners in another town had doubled up on their equity by sending relatives back with the same cart for a second loan. So he

decided to require all owners in Luuq to gather with their carts at the same time. He would then check registration numbers with owner IDs before handing out any additional loans. "All right," said Ken, "let's go count carts."

"It's still too early," Abdullah advised. "The tribal elders would be angry if you were to miss any."

Ken knew Abdullah was right—things were touchy enough without fanning the flames. The civil war among rival clans had left Somalia in chaos and virtually bankrupt.

Ken's work involved supplying small loans to viable businesses. The International Rescue Committee (IRC), a privately funded relief organization, was Ken's employer and about the only source of loans for small businesses in the country. Ken had supervised the opening of two offices. He approved loans for restaurants, chicken farms, and small manufacturers, and he won the trust of dozens of tribal elders.

Initially Ken was excited by his progress, but he missed Kim. In October he had proposed to her over the phone from the IRC's base in Kenya, and she had accepted. *Only two more months and we'll be together again,* he thought.

"All right, Abdullah," Ken said, "let's inspect that lime quarry just outside town. That'll give all the cart owners time to get here."

Ken and Mohamed, an assistant, piled into the front seat of a land cruiser next to the driver, while Abdullah and several other IRC directors and lime-quarry applicants got into the back. They headed to the countryside. There were rumors of land mines, but they followed a well-traveled track. Slowing for a herd of goats, they inched down a rutted gully. Suddenly the vehicle lurched violently, stopped, and filled with dust.

Back in Boulder, Kim was staring at Ken's picture when, inexplicably, she began to cry. *What if something terrible happens to Ken?* she wondered.

She forced herself to calm down. *Nothing's going to happen. It's all right.*

The land mine had exploded with such force that the heavy vehicle was flung into the air, gouging a three-foot-deep crater in the road when it landed. The powerful blast sent shrapnel tearing up into the cab, lodging in Ken's buttocks and thigh and severing his right leg just above the ankle. Mohamed's foot was crushed. Miraculously, the driver was unhurt.

Not feeling any pain, Ken tried crawling out the driver's door, but simply spilled onto his back. Propping what was left of his legs against the seat, Ken was horrified by what he saw. Hinged by a piece of skin, his right foot and ankle were turned completely around and lying along his shin, the bare sole toward his face. The entire top and side of his left foot were peeled open like a sardine can. He was not so much bleeding as pouring blood into pools in the Somali dust. *I don't want to die,* he thought, *not here, not like this.*

With what remained of his strength, Ken tried to inch toward his radio a few feet away, but it was no use. Then Abdullah, who had crawled from the wreck, appeared and handed Ken the radio. "Kilo romeo, kilo romeo," Ken gasped, identifying himself in phonetic code.

"Kilo romeo, we read you, over."

Ken squeezed his eyes shut in thanks. "I've run over a land mine on the road to Waajid. Several of us are badly injured."

At 7:30 P.M. on December 17, Kim paced nervously at the Geneva, Switzerland, airport. *Prepare for the worst,* she coached herself. *And don't show any shock.*

She hadn't slept since she'd received the call from the IRC the previous morning. She had driven to Ken's parents to break the news. His mother, visibly upset but calm, held Kim's hand across the kitchen table.

His father, Rob, fought back tears. Now Rob stood tensely beside Kim, waiting for the chartered flight from Kenya.

When the plane landed, Ken looked thin and drawn, his eyes sunken and ringed with dark circles. I.V. bottles, bags, and tubes dangled everywhere.

"Hey, Kim," he murmured, "they cut off my leg."

Kim stroked his forehead. "I know."

Ken was fading into a morphine fog. "So . . . do you . . . still love me?"

"Of course I love you," Kim whispered. "Just rest now."

Whoso loves

Believes the impossible.

ELIZABETH BARRETT BROWNING

There in Geneva, Kim realized the full extent of Ken's injuries. His right leg had been amputated below the knee, and his left foot looked like a slab of raw meat. Because he was not stable enough to travel, Kim and Rob remained in Geneva for five days while Ken underwent foot operations.

In unspeakable pain between morphine shots, racked with fever, and often delirious, he would bite down gently on Kim's hand to cope with the pain. Kim's world was bedpans, changing sweat-soaked sheets, then piling on blankets. She had even learned to administer his I.V.s. *My God,* she thought wearily, *if we can live through this, we can live through anything.*

Doctor David Hahn of Presbyterian Saint Luke's Hospital in Denver didn't mince words after he examined Ken. "This is one messed-up foot," said the orthopedic surgeon. "We'll be lucky to save it. Even if we do, you may never be able to use it." It was December 23, just one week after the accident.

The prognosis left Ken shaken. When the doctor left, he looked at Kim. "I know what we promised each other," he began, fighting back tears, "but you don't have to marry me."

"We're getting married," Kim said firmly. "And I don't *ever* want to hear you say that again. You think I'd marry a quitter?"

"A quitter? *Me?*" he said, now a little angry. "Okay, we're not only gonna go through with the marriage, I'm gonna walk down the aisle with you on my arm—no wheelchair, no crutches, no canes, nothing!"

"Oh, yeah?" said Kim. "What makes you think you'll be able to do that?"

" 'Cause I just made up *my* mind to," Ken answered.

They looked into each other's eyes through tears. "What did I do to deserve you?" Ken asked.

"Who said you deserved me?" was her retort.

Ken smiled, gathering Kim into his arms. For a few blissful moments he was free of pain.

Over the next six days, Doctor Hahn and a plastic surgeon performed four operations, almost reinventing Ken's left foot. Crushed bones were discarded or repositioned, tiny pieces of shrapnel delicately removed, torn ligaments repaired, and stomach muscles and thigh skin grafted.

Through it all Ken kept pushing himself. He would remind himself of the Rutherford family motto: *the alternative is not acceptable.* It was not acceptable to give up or complain. Ken barely had the strength to sit up in bed, yet he did pull-ups using a bar over his head. He doubled his prescribed physical therapy. He was in constant pain, yet he was always outwardly optimistic.

It was Kim who first noticed trouble. For weeks she had been sleeping on a cot at his side, continuing to care for him. But when she was late, he'd snap at her. Or if he needed something that was right next to his bed, he'd tell her to get it. *I understand,* she assured herself. *Ken is just demanding more of himself, as well as of me—trying to push beyond his limits.* Still, she spent hours alone, trying to recharge her energy. *I'm not sure I can take it much longer.*

After his last operation on December 28, Ken plunged into rehabilitation, lifting weights until he felt his muscles would burst. One by one the I.V. tubes were disconnected.

Doctors were still uncertain about his foot—the muscle tissue had taken but wasn't shrinking as expected, and the bones had fused into a rigid, football-shaped mass that ended in a point where his four toes met. But it was still his foot! *I've gotta walk on it for my wedding,* Ken kept repeating to himself as he hobbled along the hospital halls with a walker. *I've gotta do it for Kim.*

Ken gave the wheels of his wheelchair a few warm-up turns and then one great heave with his powerful arm muscles. He was exhilarated to be out of the hospital. Now he'd see what this old chair could do. It was February, and Ken was with Kim at a basketball game—his first outing since the accident.

Kim went to pick up the parked car after the game, leaving Ken at the top of a hill. When she pulled up to the arena, she saw Ken whizzing past at breakneck speed. Then she saw a wheel catch and turn in, and Ken was flung from the chair onto his bandaged stump.

People offered help, but Ken, moaning, tried crawling to the chair on his own. Kim practically dragged him to the car. She pushed him into the front seat, threw the chair into the trunk, jumped behind the wheel, and roared off.

"Okay, Ken, this is it!" she screamed. "I've had it! Why should I care for you if you don't care enough for yourself not to do a crazy thing like that?"

"The wheelchair . . . malfunctioned," Ken said. "That's all."

"*What?* That's the most ridiculous . . ." Kim slammed on the brakes. Now she was pounding on Ken's chest with her fists. "I am *not* going to marry you just to be a widow by the time I'm forty. I'm not!"

He tried restraining her, then broke down in tears. "Kim, forgive me. I've been selfish. I just don't want you to marry a . . ."

Kim put her fingers to his lips. "No, don't . . ."

". . . a cripple!" he cried. "I can't bear it! I *have* to walk!"

"You will walk, Ken," she said. "But even if you don't, it doesn't matter to me. Can't you see that? I'd much prefer you in a wheelchair than trying to fly out of one." She paused, then added, "You have to slow down and learn your limits—and mine."

"You mean you'll still marry me even if I can't walk down the aisle?"

"Ken?"

"Yeah?" he asked.

"Shut up."

Over the next few months Ken eased up on himself and, wisely, on his bride-to-be. He reined in his exercise schedule to recommended lengths and made slow, steady progress. He was fitted with a temporary prosthesis for his right leg, and a huge, braced shoe was designed for his swollen left foot. But he wasn't in the clear yet.

"You've developed an infection in your foot, Ken," Doctor Hahn announced one morning.

The night before, Ken's foot had developed a red spot on top, then swelled so much that his incisions began opening and bleeding. "So what does this mean?" Ken asked.

"It means we'll have to remove the infection," the doctor said. "You're scheduled for surgery in the morning."

A couple of hours after surgery, with Kim at his side, Ken breathed easy when he saw Doctor Hahn grinning. "I had to take out a lot," he said, "and you'll have another big hole in your foot, but the infection didn't go into the bone." If it had, the doctor went on to explain, there was a chance the foot would have had to come off.

Kim walked down the aisle on her father's arm. Waiting at the altar was Ken, beaming—and standing.

His foot was still swollen and painfully boxed into a big boot, and his other leg was still propped on a temporary prosthesis. But now, on September 10, 1994, the day of his dreams had arrived—nine months after the land-mine explosion.

As 250 family members and friends from around the world looked on, Ken and Kim exchanged vows. "Unlike most couples on their wedding day, they have had their love tested already," the minister said, "and they've come through shining."

Amen, thought Kim Rutherford.

After the couple were pronounced husband and wife, Ken took his first step down a stair holding Kim's arm. He faltered, and a collective gasp arose as he struggled to regain his balance. Then he slowly—proudly—made his way down the aisle with his bride on his arm.

In a successful marriage there is no such thing as one's way. There is only the way of both, only the bumpy, dusty, difficult, but always mutual path.

PHYLLIS McGINLEY

JUST TWO FOR BREAKFAST

BY

MARILYN MYERS SLADE

When my husband and I celebrated our thirty-eighth wedding anniversary at our favorite restaurant, Lenny, the piano player, asked, "How did you do it?"

I knew there was no simple answer, but as the weekend approached, I wondered if one reason might be our ritual of breakfast in bed every Saturday and Sunday.

It all started with the breakfast tray my mother gave us as a wedding gift. It had a glass top and slatted wooden side pockets for the morning paper—the kind you used to see in the movies. Mother loved her movies, and although she rarely had breakfast in bed, she held high hopes for her daughter. My adoring bridegroom took the message to heart.

Feeling guilty, I suggested we take turns. Despite grumblings—"I hate crumbs in my bed"—Sunday morning found my spouse eagerly awaiting his tray. Soon these weekend breakfasts became such a part of our lives that I never even thought about them. I only knew we treasured this separate, blissful time—to read, relax, forget the things we should remember.

Sifting through the years, I recalled how our weekends changed, but that we still preserved the ritual. We started our family (as new parents, we slept after breakfast more than we read), but we always found our way back to where we started, just two for breakfast, one on Saturday and one on Sunday.

When we had more time, my tray became more festive. First it was fruit slices placed in geometric patterns; then came flowers from our garden—sometimes just one blossom sprouting from a grapefruit half. This arranger of mine had developed a flair for decorating, using everything from amaryllis to the buds of a maple tree. He said my cooking inspired him. Mother would have approved.

Perhaps it was the Saturday when the big strawberry wore a daisy hat that I began to think, *How can I top this?* One dark winter night I woke with a vision of a snowman on a tray. That Sunday I scooped a handful of snow and in no time had my man made. With a flourish I put a miniature pinecone on his head.

As I delivered the tray, complete with a nicely frozen snowman, I waited for a reaction. There was none—but as I headed down the stairs, I heard a whoop of laughter and then, "You've won! Yes, sir, you've won the prize!"

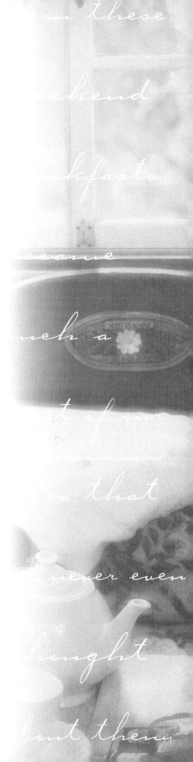

AN AFFAIR BY PHONE

BY

JAMES LEES-MILNE

In September 1941, after having been wounded in a bombing raid on London, I was discharged from the hospital. My military career had been inglorious. I was disappointed with myself, and deeply depressed by the turn the war had taken. Fortunately, at this time I was sustained by the most intimate and delicious friendship of my life.

Late one night in London I was trying to telephone a friend. Instead of getting through to him my line was crossed with that of a woman, also wanting to telephone. "My number is Grosvenor 8829," I heard her tell the operator, "and I want a Hampstead number. Instead, you have hitched me up to Flaxman something in Chelsea. This poor man doesn't want to talk to me at all."

"Oh, yes, I do," I joined in, for I liked her voice immensely. It was harmonious and clever. Instead of being cross, this woman was very good-humored about the muddle. After mutual apologies we both hung up. A minute or two later I dialed again, and again got on to her, although there was no resemblance between her number and the one I was trying to get.

Since it seemed that our lines were destined to link up, we talked for 20 minutes. "Why were you wanting to speak to a friend after midnight, anyway?" she asked. I told her the reason, which I have now forgotten. "And why were you?" I asked her. She explained that her old mother slept badly, and she often talked to her late at night. Then we discussed the books we were reading, and of course the war. Finally I said, "I don't remember enjoying a talk so much for years."

"It was fun, wasn't it? Well, I suppose we ought to stop now," she said. "Good night. Pleasant dreams."

All next day I thought of our conversation, of her intelligence, her spontaneity, her enthusiasm, her sense of fun. I thought too of her distinctive accent, which was soft and seductive, without being the least insinuating. Its musical modulation haunted me.

That evening in bed I paid little attention to what I was reading. By midnight, Grosvenor 8829 was recurring so often in my head that I could bear it no longer. I got up, and with trepidation dialed the number. I heard the swift, disengaged purr of the bell at the other end. The receiver there was picked up instantly. "Hello!"

"It's me," I said. "Sorry to be a bore, but may we continue our conversation where we left off last night?" Without saying no or yes, she launched upon a funny and original dissertation on Balzac's *La Cousine Bette*. Within minutes we were joking and laughing as though we had known each other for years.

This time we talked for three-quarters of an hour. She was enchanting. The late hour and our anonymity broke down all those absurdly conventional reserves that usually hedge two people during preliminary meetings after an introduction. But when I suggested that we ought to introduce ourselves, she would not have it. It might spoil everything, she said. Her only concession was to make a note of my telephone number.

I did extract a promise from her that we would reveal our identities when the war ended. I learned that she had been married at seventeen

to a disagreeable man from whom she was separated. She was thirty-six. Her only child had recently been killed flying at the age of eighteen. He meant everything to her and she spoke of him as though he were still alive. Since she once described him as being beautiful as the dawn, and another time as resembling her in every feature, I had a picture of her that never changed. When I told her how beautiful she was to contemplate, she merely laughed and asked, "How do you know I am?"

We grew to depend upon each other. There were no subjects we did not discuss. Our views on most were identical, including those on the war.

She gave me counsel and strength. We took to reading the same books for the fun of discussing them, and because we both belonged to the London Library each undertook not to find out from the librarians the other's name. Never a night passed when we were both in London that we did not telephone, no matter how late. I would look forward to our next talk the whole preceding day. If I went away for the weekend and was unable to telephone she complained that she could hardly get to sleep for loneliness.

At times I found it unbearable not to see her. I would threaten to jump into a taxi and drive to her at once, but she would not give in—she said that if we met and found we did not love, as then we did, it would kill her. Whenever there was a bad raid at night I would ring up, after it was over, to find out how she was. This always amused her. But I noticed that whenever she imagined there was one over Chelsea she did the same.

For 12 months I lived in an extraordinary state of inner content— extraordinary because the times through which we were living were grim, and our love was in a sense unfulfilled. But it had compensations; our passage was entirely free from the usual shoals and reefs that beset the turbulence of passion, and there seemed no reason why it should not flow on this even course forever. After all, the language of words is more powerful and more lasting than that of the eyes, or the hands.

But fate struck swiftly. One night I got back to London late from the country. I picked up the receiver and dialed her number. Instead of the clear, healthy ringing tone or the high-pitched engaged signal, there was a prolonged, piercing scream. I can never listen to that signal now without feeling faint. It means the line is out of order or no longer exists.

Next day the same scream was repeated. And the next. In distress I asked Information to find out what had happened. I begged them to give me the address of Grosvenor 8829, though I knew it was unlisted to prevent her estranged husband's unwelcome attentions.

At first Information would say nothing. They thought it odd that I could not even tell them the subscriber's name. Finally an obliging operator agreed for once to disregard regulations. "Why not?" she said. "We may all be blown sky-high any moment. And you seem worried. The fact is that the house to which this number belonged received a direct hit three days ago. There can be no harm now in giving you the subscriber's name."

"Thank you for your help," I said. "I would much rather you didn't. Please, please don't." And I rang off.

ALL HE HAD WAS HOPE

BY

LUCINDA HAHN

*U*nder the gaze of some 35,000 spectators and millions of television viewers, Donghua Li stood in front of the leather pommel horse and took a deep breath. His entire life was in this exercise, 22 years of practice in 45 seconds. He flexed his knees and began.

Donghua appeared flamelike, his swirling legs swathed in the red of the Swiss national team. It was July 28, 1996: the final day of the competition in his event at the Olympic Games in Atlanta. Donghua finished with a perfect dismount. The Georgia Dome erupted in cheers. But the gymnast forgot about the judges' score as he looked toward one face in the crowd.

Eight years earlier, on June 19, 1988, Donghua Li was pushing his bike through the streets of Beijing, near Tiananmen Square, when his eyes fell upon a flaxen-haired young tourist scrutinizing a map. She was obviously alone and looked in need of help.

"Hello?" he addressed her hesitantly in English. "Are you American? Canadian?"

"No, I'm from Switzerland," the young woman replied.

"Ah! Beautiful," he said, smiling, remembering photographs of the snowcapped Swiss Alps. They began to converse, and Donghua showed her a photo of himself on the high bar.

"You?" she asked, startled. Esperanza Friedli, twenty-three, had been a passionate gymnast as a child, and still loved the sport. But the twenty-year-old before her was a world-class athlete—the 1987 Chinese pommel-horse champion.

Through more halting exchanges, Esperanza learned that Donghua had injured two vertebrae in training and would miss the Seoul Olympic Games a few months later. He was recovering and hoped to compete four years later in the 1992 Barcelona Games. Before they parted, she agreed to visit him at his gym. "See you tomorrow," she said with a smile.

The next day Esperanza edged past the guard at the National Training Center. From the balcony she looked down at the array of equipment in the vast gym. Coaches were everywhere; physiotherapists and masseuses stood by. Esperanza marveled at how everything was taken care of, remembering the spartan gym of her childhood in Lucerne.

During the next ten days, Esperanza and Donghua strolled together in the park near the training center, went boating and to a rock concert. To communicate, they used hand gestures and dictionaries. Donghua inundated Esperanza with questions about her family and home. As they spoke, her feelings for him grew.

They discussed their names, a subject full of meaning to the Chinese. Donghua, he explained, means "flower of the East." Esperanza showed him a tourist souvenir with her name engraved in Chinese. "Hope," Donghua read, feeling a burst of happiness. He thought it might be a good sign.

When Esperanza's visit to China was over, Donghua accompanied her to the train station. "I'm sad," he said.

His entire life was in this exercise, 22 years of for in 45 seconds.

"Write to me," she replied, tears running down her cheeks. Donghua stood waving as the train shrank to a dot on the horizon, then disappeared.

In Lucerne Esperanza took a job selling furniture and thought about her smiling gymnast. "Will you remember me?" she wrote. "I miss you." Donghua translated her letters at night in the dormitory of the sports complex. "Maybe my good luck is waiting for me," he replied. Their words flew back and forth across the continents.

For the first time gymnastics alone did not satisfy Donghua. He began dreaming aloud of a future with the beautiful woman from Switzerland. Then a fellow athlete took him aside. "If you really love this girl," he said, "marry her as soon as possible." The window that had opened to the West could shut at any time, he warned.

Soon after, the phone rang at the apartment Esperanza shared with her father, brothers, and sister. It was an English-speaking woman, translating for an impatient Donghua. "Will you come to his next competition—and later get married?" she asked.

"Let me talk to him," Esperanza said, desperate to hear his voice.

When Donghua got on the telephone, she told him, "Yes, I will try to come."

In the following days, Esperanza kept her plans secret from her father, whom she knew would think the marriage rash. "I'm leaving my job," she finally told him one morning, "and returning to China."

"But what job prospects do you have in China?" Gaston Friedli asked. "It's crazy." Then he saw the determined look in his daughter's eyes. It was a determination he'd counted on when his wife had left the family, and fifteen-year-old Esperanza had helped manage the household and her four younger siblings.

In China Donghua approached the sports officials with his plans. "Love is love, and career is career," Donghua tried to argue. "One has nothing to do with the other."

The officials' answer was brief. "Marry, and your gymnastics career is finished," an administrator told him. "You have three days to decide."

Donghua was devastated. From the age of seven he had been a gymnast first, a person second. He had left his parents' household to join the sports college, and since the age of sixteen, his family had been the national team. His place on the team gave him everything he needed to achieve his dream: winning Olympic gold at the Barcelona Games in 1992.

But the day before his deadline, Donghua went to the officials. "I love gymnastics and I love Esperanza," he said. "But my love for her is more important."

On December 12, 1988, Esperanza and Donghua were married in his native city of Chengdu. Two months later the couple boarded the Trans-Siberian Express for Switzerland, where they hoped Donghua would gain a spot on the Swiss national team for the next Olympics.

They were met by Esperanza's father. *"Sali, Papi,"* Donghua said in well-rehearsed Swiss-German. He bowed respectfully.

As Gaston Friedli shook hands with his new son-in-law, his chest tightened. He wondered if his daughter understood what problems a foreigner could encounter.

When the couple first visited Lucerne's best gym, athletes flashed glances at the stranger. "My husband would like to train here," Esperanza told one of the coaches, Bruno Nietlispach.

"Is he good?" asked Bruno.

"Yes, pretty good," she replied.

Donghua mounted the pommel horse. "It's unbelievable," said one of the club's top gymnasts, awed by the long, straight line Donghua's hips and legs achieved; the quickness of his hands; the wide, high scissors he made. Nietlispach laughed in joyful astonishment.

"We had great luck that love and chance brought Donghua Li to Lucerne," he told a reporter.

Officials of the Swiss Gymnastics Federation assured Donghua that he would get on the national team, and the athlete began training while the paper work was being done.

Donghua had a big adjustment to make. The gym was sparse compared with his former surroundings. Not much bigger than a basketball court, it had just two pommel horses. Used to practicing morning and afternoon, Donghua now could not begin until 5:00 P.M.

Many waters cannot quench love, neither can floods drown it.

SONG OF SOLOMON 8

Esperanza's salary was not enough to support the two of them, and for the first time in his life, Donghua had to worry about money. He did menial work at a bus garage in Horgen, near Zurich. Every morning he woke up at 5:45 and commuted 40 minutes to his job, where he cleaned buses and moved heavy wheels. He wondered how he could stay competitive under such conditions.

Then Donghua was hit by another blow: he would not be allowed on the national team until he became a citizen—a process that in his case would take five years.

"I can't lose five years!" Donghua cried, his dream of competing in the 1992 Olympics crumbling.

"We will get over these problems," Esperanza said, taking his hand. "I believe in you." Clinging to the hope that the Swiss government would grant his citizenship early, they decided that Donghua would leave his job and concentrate solely on gymnastics. In July 1990 they moved to Biel, near the national training center. Esperanza worked in a chocolate shop to support them both.

It was a low period in his life, but Donghua did not doubt that his marriage to Esperanza had been the right choice. Indeed, he had only one real regret.

One Saturday evening Donghua turned to Esperanza in their tiny apartment. "I want to have a child with you so badly," he said, "but we can hardly afford to go to a film."

"Donghua," Esperanza said quietly, "someday we *will* have a child."

In December 1991 a letter arrived from the naturalization authorities: Donghua would have to wait the full five years. He would miss the Olympics next year. It was a staggering setback. He was already at the far edge of his gymnastic prime; by the 1996 Olympics he'd be twenty-nine. "My best years are being taken from me," he said bitterly.

During the Barcelona Games, Donghua and Esperanza watched the gymnastics competition on television. The pommel-horse event was excruciating. "I am as good as they are," he said aloud.

The couple returned to Lucerne. Esperanza went to work in a department store. Donghua trained for 1996 in the crowded gym, aided by Bruno Nietlispach, the one Swiss besides Esperanza who showed him unwavering support.

"Remember that you are the best," Bruno would tell him. Donghua stayed late in the gym most evenings, often alone, videotaping the intense practice sessions and analyzing every move.

In March 1994 Donghua received his Swiss citizenship. Two weeks later he was on a plane to Brisbane, Australia, for the 1994 World Gymnastic Championships. It was his first major event in six years, and Donghua took third place. At the 1995 World Championships in Japan, he won the gold— and the right to represent Switzerland in the Atlanta Olympics.

A TV reporter asked him how he felt. "Without the support of my wife, this would not be possible," he said. "She always believed in me." Watching from home, Esperanza wept.

But on the horizon of the gymnastic world, new, younger competitors were rising. Some experts argued that twenty-nine-year-old Donghua was too old to win at the Olympic Games. Donghua ignored his detractors. He had a secret to sustain his spirit: the woman named Hope was carrying their child.

Donghua stayed calm under the glare of Olympic pressure, but the day before the final event, he woke up with a sore throat and fever. "I don't feel so well," he told Bruno, shivering.

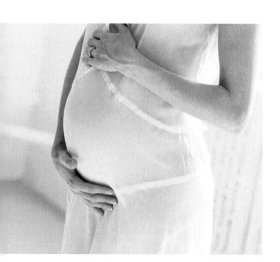

The team doctor examined him, then spoke privately with the coach. "He has serious tonsillitis," the doctor said. Bruno nodded sagely and returned to Donghua. "Good news," Bruno said, smiling. "It's only a cold. Tomorrow you'll feel fine."

The next day a still-feverish Donghua and his competitors marched into the Georgia Dome. Spotting Esperanza in the crowd, he waved.

While the first competitors performed, Donghua lay facedown on a mat and visually rehearsed his exercise. He knew that he faced strong competition. Only mental toughness would enable him to win.

Flexing his shoulders to keep his muscles loose, he vaguely heard the crowd's reactions to his competitors' scores. But when he got up to prepare for his routine, he had no idea that Romania's Marius Urzica had scored a nearly perfect 9.825 out of 10.

Finally Donghua stood facing the pommel horse. Esperanza watched with her hands clasped and pressed against her lips. "You can do it, Donghua," she whispered.

Donghua mounted the pommel horse. Working from one end to the other, he cemented his legs together in perfect form. Then he spread them into a V, and they helicoptered powerfully about his torso. After the dismount Donghua looked to Esperanza in the crowd. He breathed deeply: he'd done his best.

Then his score appeared: 9.875!

"Ja!" Esperanza yelled in delight. Donghua clenched his fists in triumph.

After the medal presentation, Esperanza and Donghua clutched each other in a long embrace. Then Donghua took his gold medal and rubbed it against his wife's belly.

"Esperanza gave me her heart," he told the press. "Then she gave me the way from Switzerland to Atlanta. Now she is giving me a child. This medal is for her and for our baby."

THE LOVES WE LEAVE BEHIND

BY

LISA BAIN

My father met my mother in a poker game. He said she was the best bluffer he'd ever seen. She sat with five men at a table under an elm tree that shaded them from the hot Kansas City, Missouri, sun. Her talent for subterfuge lay hidden behind her sweet, serene smile. She beat them all. My father couldn't take his eyes off her.

It was her company's annual picnic, and he walked her home. The next week, from his home in Chicago, he sent her a postcard: "Remember me? Please do, 'cause I'll be calling you one of these days. David."

She still has that postcard. I'm not sure what made her save it. Though he already had his heart set on her, she hadn't chosen him yet, at least not consciously.

As my father often told us while we were growing up, it was blind luck that he was at the picnic that day. A salesman for a big electronics company, he was in town to meet with clients and happened to stop by the branch office that Saturday morning to make some calls. The telephone rang: it was the manager of a local radio station with whom my father had done some business. "Dave! Glad you're in town!" he said, and invited him to come right over to their annual picnic.

My mother was a writer at that radio station. If my father hadn't stopped by the office that morning, he told us, or if he'd gotten there two minutes later . . . We shivered with a delicious horror at the opportunity, the life—*our* lives—that would have been missed.

My mother saw him when he was in town, but she dated other men, including a car salesman who entered our family lore. Soon after she met my father, the car salesman gave her a watch for her birthday. In those days the gift of a watch meant the relationship was moving toward an engagement. But she returned the watch, and one night a few months later, she woke her mother and told her she was going to marry Dave.

A few months after the wedding, my father was transferred East. They settled in New York, in the house where I grew up.

I was eight years old when I met *my* future husband. He was in high school, a friend of my brother's. I remember him only peripherally, as I was much more interested in my brother's *other* friend—François, a Swiss exchange student, dark, mysterious, and polished.

Fifteen years later the man I would eventually marry came back to town for Christmas and stopped by my parents' house to pick up my brother for an evening out. When he saw me in the next room, he hissed, "Who's *that?*"

My brother looked at him strangely and said, "It's just Lisa."

He walked into the room, reintroduced himself, and pretended he didn't know how to wrap his Christmas gifts. I pretended to believe him and helped. He came around a lot over the next few days. "I don't know who he's interested in," my mother told me, "you or your sister." I knew. But later that week I flew across the country to spend New Year's Eve with another man. Though I'd been chosen, I wasn't ready to admit it yet.

If the timing had been different, the distance less daunting, and my heart not already—albeit unknowingly—engaged, I could have ended up with that man whom I went off to visit. Or if not him, then with someone else.

Sometimes I think about that, how time sweeps us along and puts us in a certain place where we're faced with one option or another. By chance and by the choices we make, we leave behind whole other lives we could have lived, full of different passions and joys, different problems and disappointments.

My father could have missed that picnic. Or my mother could have picked the car salesman. She would have had other children and an entirely different future.

Other times—particularly when I come home late to a sleeping house, my husband and daughter curled around each other after drifting off during the third reading of Jane Yolen's *Owl Moon*—I think about the lives we would not have had if chance or choice had brought us to a different place. And I shiver, much the way I did as a child at the story of my father's near miss, at the thought that I might have missed *this* life, this man, this child, this love.

Love is a fruit in season at all times, and

within the reach of every hand.

MOTHER TERESA OF CALCUTTA

AN EVENING AT THE WALDORF

BY

JEAN AND BUD INCE

Bud: One rainy October evening, 30 years ago, I sat in my room at the Naval Academy in Annapolis, staring at a navigation lesson and thinking of Jean. I had met her the previous August in Chicago and had fallen in love. Three days later I was back in Annapolis, surrounded by rules and regulations, while she was a thousand miles away, surrounded by eligible bachelors. Things looked bleak, indeed.

There was one bright spot on the horizon. Jean was coming to Philadelphia for the Army-Navy game in November. We had been invited to spend the weekend with my uncle and aunt in New York. If there was any hope for me, that weekend was going to have to be one she would never forget. I shoved my books aside and wrote the following letter:

The Manager
The Waldorf-Astoria
New York City, New York

Dear Sir:

On Saturday, November 27, I expect to pick my way across the prostrate bodies of the West Point football team to a seat in Municipal Stadium where a girl will be waiting. We will hie away to the railroad station and entrain for New York. Once there we will take a taxi to your hotel—and that, dear sir, is where you and the Waldorf-Astoria come in.

I am very much in love with this young lady, but she has not yet admitted to an equivalent love for me. Trapped as I am in this military monastery, the chances I have to press my suit are rare indeed. Therefore, this evening must be the most marvelous of all possible evenings, for I intend to ask her to be my wife.

I would like a perfect table. There should be candlelight, gleaming silver, and snowy linen. There should be wine and a dinner that will be the culmination of the chef's career. At precisely midnight, I would like the orchestra to play "Navy Blue and Gold" very softly.

And then I intend to propose.

I would appreciate it very much if you could confirm this plan and also tell me approximately what the bill will be. I am admittedly not getting rich on $13 a month, but I have put a little aside.

Very truly yours,
E. S. Ince
Midshipman, U.S.N.

The minute the letter was gone I regretted having sent it. It was callow, smart-alecky, and, above all, presumptuous. The manager of the most famous hotel in the world was certainly not interested in the love life of an obscure midshipman. The letter would be thrown into the wastebasket where it belonged.

One week went by and then another. I forgot about the letter and tried frantically to think of some other way to convince Jean in 36 hours that she should spend the rest of her life with me. Then one morning I found on my desk an envelope upon which was engraved "The Waldorf-Astoria." I tore it open and read:

Dear Midshipman Ince:

Your very nice letter has been receiving some attention from our staff here. Just for fun I am going to attach the suggestions of our Maître d', the famous René Black.

"Black pearls of the Sturgeon from the Caspian Sea, stuffed into the claws of lobsters, and eulogizing the God of the Oceans.

"The Filet of Pompano known as the Demoiselle of the Atlantic, placed in a paper bag with the nomenclature 'Greetings from the Poseidon.'

"The Breast of Chicken served in a little nest to represent the safety of the ketch, with its escort of vegetables and green salad.

"An excellent dessert bearing the nomenclature 'Ritorna vincitor' from Aida, and little galettes. A sweet liqueur to seal the anticipation.

"The price of this manoeuvre, *including wines, champagne, gratuities, flowers, and music, will be in the vicinity of $100, with which we hope your little cache is fortified for complete victory."*

Frankly, unless you have private resources, I think it is entirely unnecessary to spend so much money. I would be happy to make a reservation for you in the Wedgwood Room and will see to it that you have a very nice table, the best of attention, flowers—and you and your girl order directly from the menu whatever intrigues you. You certainly can have a couple of cocktails and very nice dinners and a bottle of champagne for one-third of what René Black

suggests. However, you are the only one who can make the decision so let me
know how you would like to have us arrange your little party.

Best wishes.

Cordially yours,
Henry B. Williams
Manager

P.S. I think your delightful letter inspired our Mr. Black.

I was thunderstruck with excitement and gratitude. But also dismayed. I didn't have even close to $100 saved. Regretfully, I wrote Mr. Williams that he had made a closer estimate of my resources than had Mr. Black, and I would appreciate it if he would reserve a table for me.

Days went by with no confirmation of my reservation. I was sure that my letter had never reached Mr. Williams, or that the whole thing had been taken as a joke. Finally, it was the weekend of November 27. The Brigade of Midshipmen watched their inspired team hold highly favored Army to a 21–21 tie in a thrilling football game. Afterward, I rushed to meet Jean, and she was just as pretty and wonderful as I had remembered her.

On the train to New York I showed Jean the letter from Mr. Williams. I told her that I wasn't sure we had a reservation, or whether we should even go to the Waldorf. We decided that we should.

We walked into the lobby. To the right, at the top of some steps, was the Wedgwood Room. There was a velvet rope at the bottom of the steps, and another at the top, with a major-domo posted at both places. A crowd of fashionably dressed couples was waiting for admittance. I looked at Jean, and she at me. Finally, I gulped, "Here goes," and went fearfully up to the first major-domo. "Sir," I said, "I am Midshipman Ince, and I wonder if you happen to have a reservation for me."

Like magic he swept away the rope! "Indeed we do," he said, and we saw the headwaiter at the top of the steps smiling and saying, "Midshipman Ince?" "Yes, sir," I managed. "Right this way," he said, and snapped his fingers. A captain led us across the room toward a beautiful table. Two waiters were leaning over it, lighting tall white candles . . .

Jean: Walking ahead of Bud, I looked in amazement at the table. Centered between the candles in a low white vase were flowers—white stephanotis and pink sweetheart roses. When the red-coated waiter seated me I saw a box at my place. I opened it and found a corsage of white baby orchids.

The menu was hand-painted in watercolor. A gray Navy ship steamed toward the upper right-hand corner, and high-lighted on the left was a sketch of a girl's head with blue love-birds in her hair.

At the moment our excitement over the flowers, the table, and the menu had subsided to a point admitting of intrusion, our waiter said to Bud, "Would you like a cocktail?"

We agreed that we would like a Manhattan, and that was the only question we were asked all evening.

The dinner began. Silver sparkled and crystal glistened in the candle-light. Eddy Duchin and his orchestra played in the background. Service was constant, attentive, unobtrusive, and each course was more lovely than the one that came before it.

About halfway through our dinner a distinguished gentleman with silvery-gray hair and a large Gallic nose approached our table. "I am René Black. I just came over to make sure that you were not angry with me." Bud leaped to his feet and I beamed, as we poured out our thanks to the man who had planned this evening. He drew up a chair and sat

All mankind loves a lover.

RALPH WALDO EMERSON

down and talked, delighting us with anecdotes of his continuing love affair with his wife and of the origin of omelets, and a wonderful tale of a dinner party he gave his regiment in France during World War I. When we asked him if he had painted the menu, he smiled, turned it over, and quickly sketched the head of a chef with his pen. Under it he wrote, *"Si l'amour ne demande que des baisers à quoi bon la gloire de cuisinier?"* (If love requires only kisses, of what use is the fame of the cook?)

After Mr. Black left, I looked at Bud. I had made plans to come to see the Army-Navy game and to spend the weekend with him. But I wondered how I would feel about the dashing midshipman I had met so briefly last summer.

Now, here we were in the Waldorf-Astoria in New York. We had just talked with the famous René Black; we had been served a dinner to delight royalty and were sipping wine together. How wonderful!

Bud: A few moments later Eddy Duchin left his bandstand and came to our table. The legendary orchestra leader was warm and friendly as he talked about the great game Navy had played that afternoon; he himself had served in the Navy during World War II. When Jean's attention was distracted for a moment, he leaned over to me and whispered, " 'Navy Blue and Gold' at midnight. Good luck!" He rose, grinning, and walked back to his piano.

We were sipping a liqueur when the waiter told me there was a telephone call for me in the lobby. I followed him, wondering who in the world could be calling, only to find the headwaiter waiting just outside the door. He handed me the bill and said, "We thought you might prefer not to have this brought to your table." I turned it over fearfully and looked at the total. It was $33—exactly what I had written Mr. Williams I could afford. It was clear to me that this amount couldn't even begin to cover the cost of the evening to the Waldorf, and equally clear that the reason the bill was presented with such finesse was to save me embarrassment had I not had $33. I looked at the headwaiter in amazement, and he smiled and said, "Everyone on the staff hopes that all goes well for you."

Jean: Bud came back to the table gleaming, and, in answer to my curiosity about the telephone call, said, "It was nothing important. Shall we dance?" I felt his hand on my arm, guiding me gently to the dance floor. Other couples danced about us, chatting and smiling. I saw only Bud. We were living a fairy-tale evening, and it was all real. "I'm in love!" I thought. "How wonderful. I'm in love."

Bud: At five minutes till midnight, we were sitting at our table in a glow of happiness. Suddenly the wine steward appeared at my side with a small bottle of champagne. He opened it with a subdued "pop" and filled two crystal goblets with the sparkling wine. I raised my glass to Jean, and at that moment the orchestra drummer ruffled his drums. Eddy Duchin turned to us and bowed. He raised his hand and brought it down; suddenly we heard the melody of that most beautiful and sentimental of all college alma maters. ". . . For sailormen in battle fair since fighting days of old have proved the sailor's right to wear the Navy Blue and Gold." I looked at Jean, my wonderful Jean, and with a lump in my throat said, "Will you marry me?"

Jean: Bud and I were married the following June. Now, with our five children grown and the Midshipman a Rear Admiral, we sometimes turn the pages of the lovely wedding gift we received from Mr. Williams—a handsomely bound limited edition of the history of the Waldorf-Astoria. In it one can read of the princes and potentates, presidents and kings, who have been guests of that glamorous hotel. But there is one evening that is not included there—an evening in which kind, warm-hearted, gently romantic men opened a door of happiness for a young couple in love. That evening is ours, and its testimony is Mr. Black's wedding gift. Framed and displayed in a place of honor on our dining-room wall, it is a watercolor sketch of a little chef tending his spit in an ancient kitchen. Printed in Mr. Black's familiar hand across the top, the words are repeated:

Si l'amour
ne demande que des baisers
à quoi bon
la gloire de cuisinier

Love does not consist in gazing at each other,
but in looking outward together in the same
direction.

ANTOINE DE SAINT-EXUPERY

"HELLO, YOUNG LOVERS"

BY

PHILIP HARSHAM

He appeared almost Lilliputian, dwarfed by the big hickory rocking chair he occupied on the porch of the old Riverside Hotel in Gatlinburg, Tennessee. But we could hardly help noticing him on that warm mid-April day: while others lounged about in casual attire, he wore a dark-blue pin-stripe suit, a Harvard-crimson necktie, and a straw boater. The gold watch chain draped across his tightly buttoned vest glinted in the sunlight as he rocked ever so deliberately.

He watched bemusedly as I stepped from the Jaguar XK-150, my pride and joy, and walked to the opposite side to open the door for my bride. His eyes followed as we trailed self-consciously behind the luggage-laden bellboy, and he smiled a knowing smile when we neared his rocker.

"Hello, young lovers," he said. Our honeymooner status was unmistakable.

The man we came to know as Mr. B was in the dining room, sitting alone with a cup of tea, when we entered late the next morning. His eyes came to life when he saw us. He rose with some effort and beckoned us toward him.

"You'd make an old man very happy if you joined me," he said with an octogenarian's formality. I wonder even now why we did. Perhaps it was the angelic expression his face assumed. More likely, it was our honeymooner self-consciousness; we'd been found out by an elder and felt compelled to comply with his wishes.

He was a Canadian, an attorney, he said, still practicing in Winnipeg. But he'd been spending Aprils in Gatlinburg for almost 50 years. He and his wife would come with their son and daughter and explore the mountains on horseback, getting to know every scenic vantage point of Mount Le Conte, every turn in the tumbling Little Pigeon River.

After the son had died and after the daughter was grown, Mr. B and his wife had kept up their visits. And he still continued to make the annual trek even though his wife had died three years ago. The mountains and the valley were touchstones for him, sites of pleasant memories that were revived with each visit.

"I've had a love of my own," he said, his eyes misting. He asked detailed questions about our wedding and told us in detail of his own, some 60 years earlier. During brief periods when a conversational lapse threatened, he softly hummed "Hello, Young Lovers," the song from *The King and I.*

That night he sat alone during dinner, careful, he later told us, not to "get in love's way." But he glanced often in our direction, and we knew he was not alone; he was deep in reverie, dining with his own true love. Returning to our room following an after-dinner walk, we found a ribbon-bedecked bottle of champagne. An accompanying card read: "See Mr. B in the a.m. for instructions as to its use."

He was waiting for us in his rocking chair after breakfast, the look of a leprechaun on his face. He handed me a piece of paper on which he had sketched the river, a place where we could leave our car, a footpath, and points at which large boulders made it possible to cross the

cold mountain stream on foot. His shaky-handed path led eventually to a river pool indicated with an X.

"The champagne is to be chilled in the pool," he said. "You are to spread your picnic lunch on the grassy knoll to the right of it. It's very secluded. A very romantic spot." We could only gape at him, certain he was spoofing.

"Your picnic basket will be delivered to you here on the veranda at precisely noon." He was on his feet then, moving away. He turned and added: "It was our favorite spot, our secret place."

We never saw Mr. B again during our honeymoon. We wondered whether he'd fallen ill. But inquiries to the hotel staff were answered with, "Oh, he's around," or "He often likes to be alone."

Our firstborn was almost three when we next visited Gatlinburg, and my wife was six months pregnant with our second son. We approached the aging hotel not in the Jaguar, but in a practical sedan. Our arrival went unnoticed.

But when we walked into the hotel lobby the next morning, our son toddling ahead, the old man was sitting in an overstuffed lounge chair. Seeing the child, he stretched out his arms, and our son, as if drawn by a magnet, ran into them.

"Mr. B!" we exclaimed in unison.

He smiled that beatific smile. "Hello, young lovers," he said.

Love is like a violin. The music may stop

now and then, but the strings remain forever.

JUNE MASTERS BACHER

"I'VE NEVER FORGOTTEN"

BY
LAWRANCE THOMPSON

The poet Robert Frost frequently told me about his first love. She was, he said, a dark-haired, dark-eyed, mischievous tomboy. Her name was Sabra Peabody and she and Frost had been schoolmates, many years before, in Salem, New Hampshire. As an awkward twelve-year-old he wrote her ardent notes, but the young lady had many other admirers and did not encourage him. Eventually he moved away from the village and heard no more from her.

As Frost's official biographer, I mentally filed this information. But I did nothing about it until years later, when I heard that the same Sabra Peabody, now a widow, had returned to Salem to live. I wrote for an interview and received a cordial invitation from her to come to call.

I was received by a tall, lithe, vibrant woman in her seventies, white-haired, and still beautiful. Her memories about the school days with Frost were much like those the elderly poet had given me. She told me how she, her brother Charles, and "Rob" used to roam the woods together after school and on Saturdays. Adventurous like her brother,

116

she used to tease Frost into keeping pace with them. She recalled that he sometimes quarreled with her over her other beaux.

I did not stay long that day, but was encouraged to return. It was during my second visit that the unexpected happened—the kind of thing biographers dream of but seldom encounter.

We had talked again, even more freely than before. Finally I stood to take my leave. Sabra remained seated. "Was there something else?" I asked. Yes, said Sabra, she had just been waiting for the right moment. She told me that this house, to which she had returned after her husband's death, had been her childhood home. Recently she had opened a dusty steamer trunk in the attic and found several family keepsakes, among them a wooden pencil box she had used in grammar-school days.

Holding it in her hand, she had suddenly remembered that in the bottom of the box there was a secret compartment that could be opened by sliding the thin wooden base outward. She tried it, the secret compartment opened, and out feel four notes, notes written by "Rob" to Sabra, perhaps in the fall of 1886. She now wanted me to see them.

As she took the notes out of a desk drawer and gave them to me, I felt great excitement in the knowledge that, almost by accident, I held the earliest known writing of a major literary figure. But as I began to read I found further rewards. "I like those leavs you gave me and put them in my speller to press," one note started out. Another pleaded: "There is no fun in getting mad every so often so lets see if we cant keep friends . . . I like you because I cant help myself and when I get mad at you I feel mad at myself to." In such lines I could sense the rapture and the anguish of a boy in love.

The former Sabra Peabody had no idea of the importance of this find. When she offered to give me the notes, I explained that their market value was too high for me to accept them as a gift. But would she consider donating them to the collection of Robert Frost's papers at the Jones Public Library in Amherst, Massachusetts?

She agreed, and I delivered them a few days later to Charles R. Green, curator of the collection. Since I feared that the poet might not approve of my snooping, I asked that this gift be kept a secret. I further requested that the notes be matted, with backing, and wrapped in heavy paper; that the package be tied with string, and placed in the vault of the library with the notation "Not to Be Opened During Robert Frost's Lifetime." The secret might have been preserved as planned, had not fate intervened—in the person of Robert Frost himself!

Frost had stored in that same vault a small metal strongbox containing manuscripts of some early poems. Shortly after the four notes had been turned over to the library, he appeared there unexpectedly to retrieve one of the poems. Green offered to bring the box out, but Frost said time could be saved if they both went into the vault. The poet opened his strongbox, took what he wanted, closed it—and looked around. "What's this?" he asked.

Green had inadvertently placed the secret package on a nearby shelf. Frost peered at it, then read aloud, "Not to Be Opened During Robert Frost's Lifetime." He turned accusingly to the curator. "This is your handwriting, Mr. Green."

Flustered, Green said yes, yes it was, but Larry Thompson had asked him to write it because . . .

Frost was in no mood for explanations. With clenched hands he broke the string, then tore the wrapping off the package. After reading the notes carefully, the old gentleman shoved the material back on the shelf. Then he turned and, without a word to anyone, stalked out of the library.

Green's letter of apology gave me all the details and said that the poet seemed very angry. I was worried. If Frost should not forgive me for my snooping without his permission, my work on the biography might end before it really began. What could I do to make amends? Perhaps it would be best, I decided, to let his anger cool, even to wait until *he* chose to bring up the subject. I waited.

Nothing happened until the following June when I arrived in Vermont to spend some time with the poet as he and I had planned. When I reached his farm, he was in his vegetable garden setting out a row of lettuce seedlings. His greeting was cordial and his instructions were sensible: I should take off my city jacket and prove my farming background by helping him get these plants into the ground before they began to wilt. After we finished, we went up to his cabin and sat down before the stone fireplace. Frost began to tell me how a fox had made off with one of his hens. "I didn't react fast enough," he said. "Nothing like that has happened to me since I was a boy in Salem and . . ."

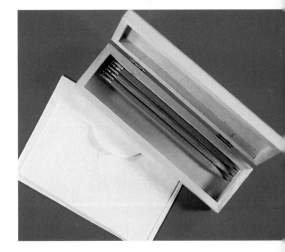

Salem! Reminded of unfinished business, he stopped in the middle of the sentence. His expression changed. He leaned toward me, shook the index finger of his right hand under my nose, and said, "You! You! What *you* did to *me!*" With that he launched into his version of the visit to the Jones Library.

He said that as soon as he saw the admonition on the packet and heard Green say my name, he knew that I'd been prying. Hurt and angry that I hadn't confided in him, he had broken the string and torn open the package almost before he realized what he was doing.

The feeling of resentment had been swept away by the opening words: "Dear Sabe." No one could possibly understand, he said, how overwhelmed he was by the memories that flooded up as he read. By the time he finished the last note, he could feel the tears burning in his eyes. He couldn't bear to have Green see those tears; he couldn't talk to anyone. So he fled. When Frost paused and silence filled the room, I was the one whose eyes stung.

Then, suddenly, his manner changed and he looked me straight in the eye. "So you found her?" he asked quietly.

I nodded.

"Where?"

"Salem."

He continued to stare at me and I didn't dare go on. The silence became uncomfortable. Finally he spoke, almost to himself. "Sixty years!" I had to lean forward to hear him. "Sixty years . . . and I've never forgotten."

Then he leaned back. "You can start," he said quietly. "Start at the beginning and tell me all about her."

Two such as you with such a master speed

Cannot be parted nor swept away

From one another once you are agreed

That life is only life forevermore

Together wing to wing and oar to oar.

ROBERT FROST

MY HUSBAND'S HANDS

BY

HELEN TROISI ARNEY

*P*aul's hands were twice as long as mine and half a hand wider. His fingers did not taper; they were long and square, laced with fine veins all the way to the tips. His nails squared off the ends of his fingers, with clearly defined moons and white edges. He took great pride in keeping them neat.

My husband's hands had a fine firm feeling, warm, never cold, never moist. And in his final days, when he pressed them both together around one of my hands, I closed my eyes and concentrated on memorizing the feeling.

Had I remembered to tell him that I found his large hands beautiful? Did I ever explain that in his clasp in a movie, in church, I felt pure and honest expressions of his love?

Those hands gave our newborn daughter her first bath and did the same for the five babies who followed. They gave haircuts to three sons and toweled three daughters' hair after showers.

Those hands were not tough hands, or soft either. They were the hands of a college professor, and they traced patterns in the air as he taught marketing students at the university where he himself had studied so many years earlier.

Those hands stripped and refinished furniture. They cut and refashioned the metal sides of an outgrown children's swimming pool, then used them to mend fenders and rust spots of secondhand cars. They manipulated suitcases atop station wagons for 28 summer pilgrimages to visit grandparents in Pennsylvania.

Those hands reached for mine through months of chemotherapy and radiation. They clasped mine in the deepest, darkest moment when he whispered into the curve of my neck, "I wonder how it is to die. I wonder if it hurts."

And those hands flailed in unconscious confusion as he spoke to his own father, who had died years earlier: "Daddy, I can't lift my legs. Daddy, I can't move my arms. Daddy, sometimes I'm hot and sometimes I'm cold."

I asked, "Is your father trying to help you through this?" There was no answer but the stillness of his listenings as all movement stopped.

"I'll be all right," I said. "We'll be all right. I think you should take your daddy's hand and let him lead you."

Early Wednesday morning, in a state of nervous anxiety, I clipped, filed, and whitened his fingernails. There was no movement, no recognition, no response as I laid his hands across his chest. Within an hour the hospice nurse checked him with her stethoscope, and there was nothing left for me to do but close his luminous green eyes and lay my hands on his for the last time.

For 7½ months my grief had been frozen like an icy presence that would not yield. Then one Sunday I opened the top drawer of Paul's dresser and reached in for one of his clean, pressed handkerchiefs—I like to use them now. What I touched was an opened pack of emery boards.

I was undone. Tears came as I closed my eyes and tried to remember the clasp of Paul's hands. My grief brought to mind the funeral, when the children left to return to their own homes: Cathy to Milwaukee; Bill to San Francisco; Mary and her husband, Joe, to Sterling, Illinois; Terri and her husband, Don, to Huntington Beach, California; Michael to New York City. And Stephen, the youngest, to Bloomington, Illinois.

Stephen had kissed me good-bye and then, impulsively, had taken my hand in both of his. It was as though his father's long, graceful hands had clasped mine once again.

'Tis sweet to know there is an eye will mark

Our coming, and look brighter when we come.

LORD BYRON

LETTER IN THE WALLET

BY

ARNOLD FINE

It was a freezing day, several years ago, when I stumbled on a wallet in the street. There was no identification inside. Just three dollars, and a crumpled letter that looked as if it had been carried around for years.

The only thing legible on the torn envelope was the return address. I opened the letter and saw that it had been written in 1924—almost 60 years ago. I read it carefully, hoping to find some clue to the identity of the wallet's owner.

It was a "Dear John" letter. The writer, in a delicate script, told the recipient, whose name was Michael, that her mother forbade her to see him again. Nevertheless, she would always love him. It was signed Hannah.

It was a beautiful letter. But there was no way, beyond the name Michael, to identify the owner. Perhaps if I called information the operator could find the phone number for the address shown on the envelope.

"Operator, this is an unusual request. I'm trying to find the owner of a wallet I found. Is there any way you could tell me the phone number for an address that was on a letter in the wallet?"

I read it

carefully,

hoping

find

one else

the

tly

the

wallet's

The operator gave me her supervisor, who said there was a phone listed at the address, but that she could not give me the number. However, she would call and explain the situation. Then, if the party wanted to talk, she would connect me. I waited a minute and she came back on the line. "I have a woman who will speak with you."

I asked the woman if she knew a Hannah.

"Oh, of course! We bought this house from Hannah's family thirty years ago."

"Would you know where they could be located now?" I asked.

"Hannah had to place her mother in a nursing home years ago. Maybe the home could help you track down the daughter."

The woman gave me the name of the nursing home. I called and found out that Hannah's mother had died. The woman I spoke with gave me an address where she thought Hannah could be reached.

I phoned. The woman who answered explained that Hannah herself was now living in a nursing home. She gave me the number. I called and was told, "Yes, Hannah is with us."

I asked if I could stop by to see her. It was almost 10:00 P.M. The director said Hannah might be asleep. "But if you want to take a chance, maybe she's in the day room watching television."

The director and a guard greeted me at the door of the nursing home. We went up to the third floor and saw the nurse, who told us that Hannah was indeed watching TV.

We entered the day room. Hannah was a sweet, silver-haired old-timer with a warm smile and friendly eyes. I told her about finding the wallet and showed her the letter. The second she saw it, she took a deep breath. "Young man," she said, "this letter was the last contact I had with Michael." She looked away for a moment, then said pensively, "I loved him very much. But I was only sixteen and my mother felt I was too young. He was so handsome. You know, like Sean Connery, the actor."

We both laughed. The director then left us alone. "Yes, Michael Goldstein was his name. If you find him, tell him I still think of him often. I never did marry," she said, smiling through tears that welled up in her eyes. "I guess no one ever matched up to Michael . . ."

I thanked Hannah, said good-bye, and took the elevator to the first floor. As I stood at the door, the guard asked, "Was the old lady able to help you?"

I told him she had given me a lead. "At least I have a last name. But I probably won't pursue it further for a while." I explained that I had spent almost the whole day trying to find the wallet's owner.

While we talked, I pulled out the brown-leather case with its red-lanyard lacing and showed it to the guard. He looked at it closely and said, "Hey, I'd know that anywhere. That's Mr. Goldstein's. He's always losing it. I found it in the hall at least three times."

"Who's Mr. Goldstein?" I asked.

"He's one of the old-timers on the eighth floor. That's Mike Goldstein's wallet, for sure. He goes out for a walk quite often."

I thanked the guard and ran back to the director's office to tell him what the guard had said. He accompanied me to the eighth floor. I prayed that Mr. Goldstein would be up.

"I think he's still in the day room," the nurse said. "He likes to read at night . . . a darling old man."

We went to the only room that had lights on, and there was a man reading a book. The director asked him if he had lost his wallet.

Michael Goldstein looked up, felt his back pocket, and then said, "Goodness, it *is* missing."

"This kind gentleman found a wallet. Could it be yours?"

The second he saw it, he smiled with relief. "Yes," he said, "that's it. Must have dropped it this afternoon. I want to give you a reward."

"Oh, no thank you," I said. "But I have to tell you something. I read the letter in the hope of finding out who owned the wallet."

The smile on his face disappeared. "You read that letter?"

"Not only did I read it, I think I know where Hannah is."

He grew pale. "Hannah? You know where she is? How is she? Is she still as pretty as she was?"

I hesitated.

"Please tell me!" Michael urged.

"She's fine, and just as pretty as when you knew her."

"Could you tell me where she is? I want to call her tomorrow." He grabbed my hand and said, "You know something? When that letter came, my life ended. I never married. I guess I've always loved her."

"Michael," I said. "Come with me."

The three of us took the elevator to the third floor. We walked toward the day room where Hannah was sitting, still watching TV. The director went over to her.

"Hannah," he said softly. "Do you know this man?" Michael and I stood waiting in the doorway.

She adjusted her glasses, looked for a moment, but didn't say a word.

"Hannah, it's Michael. Michael Goldstein. Do you remember?"

"Michael? Michael? It's you!"

He walked slowly to her side. She stood and they embraced. Then the two of them sat on a couch, held hands, and started to talk. The director and I walked out, both of us crying.

"See how the good Lord works," I said philosophically. "If it's meant to be, it will be."

Three weeks later, I got a call from the director, who asked, "Can you break away on Sunday to attend a wedding?"

He didn't wait for an answer. "Yup, Michael and Hannah are going to tie the knot!"

It was a lovely wedding, with all the people at the nursing home join-ing in the celebration. Hannah wore a beige dress and looked beautiful. Michael wore a dark-blue suit and stood tall. The home gave them their own room, and if you ever wanted to see a seventy-six-year-old bride and a seventy-eight-year-old groom acting like two teenagers, you had to see this couple.

A perfect ending for a love affair that had lasted nearly 60 years.

Love is nature's second sun.

GEORGE CHAPMAN

CAULIFLOWER LOVE

BY

ERMA BOMBECK

*W*e looked a little ridiculous—two forty-seven-year-old adults sitting alone at a card table in the backyard with party hats strapped under our chins.

It wasn't the way I had imagined our twenty-fifth wedding anniversary gala.

I had fantasized a large white tent decorated with flowers and housing a six-piece orchestra. Several hundred guests would be milling around. My husband and I would exchange diamond-studded matching tennis bracelets. He would romantically feed me out-of-season blueberries, and the orchestra would play our favorite song, "Our Love Is Here to Stay," while we swayed together on the dance floor.

Later, we would throw streamers from the deck of a cruise ship and swill champagne while our misty-eyed children waved from the pier.

The reality was, our kids had thrown a couple of hamburgers and a few hot dogs on the grill, scarfed them down, and split, leaving us to clean up. The table held our bounty: matching one-size-fits-all bathrobes and a shower booster from my husband with five positions ranging from gentle spray to pin-you-against-the-wall.

Twenty-five years. There had been a time when we would have gotten a standing ovation for being married that long. Not anymore.

Kids looked at you like you were some kind of prehistoric animal. Your contemporaries shook their heads in disgust and whispered to one another, "She'd leave him in a minute, but she's too out of shape to shop."

When I read the Sunday paper, I found myself turning frequently to the section of anniversaries, people who had survived 50 or 60 years of marriage. In some strange way they were my future, sitting side by side, not touching, staring straight at the camera. Her hair was thin with a touch of pink scalp showing through. So was his. They wore matching glasses.

I knew it would only be a matter of time before no one would be able to tell us apart. Already our ideas, our stories, our ideology, and our attitudes had blended to such a degree we barely knew where one began and the other left off. Whenever he told a joke, I knew the exact moment he was going to say, "Help me with the punch line, honey."

Mentally, I checked the list of things I was going to change about him 25 years ago. He was still late all the time and still left-handed. He was with his cronies less, but had replaced them with other distractions like jogging and fishing. I threw him a vegetable or two every week and he was satisfied he was eating healthy.

I wondered for the first time if he had made such a list of my annoyances and what kind of progress he had made.

Bill scraped the last hamburger from the grill. "You want this?"

I popped it in my mouth.

"This is nice," he said.

"Did you know that Richard Burton bought Liz a rare diamond and she bought him a full-length fur coat?"

"What would I do with a fur coat in Phoenix?" he snorted.

I looked at him as he returned the folding chairs to their original boxes. We had gone through three wars, two miscarriages, five houses, three children, nine cars, 23 funerals, seven camping trips, 12 jobs, 19 banks, and three credit unions. I had cut his hair, and turned 33,488 pieces of his underwear right side out. He had washed my feet when I was pregnant and couldn't see them and put his car seat back to its original position 18,675 times after I had used it.

We had shared toothpaste, debts, closets, and relatives. We had given one another honesty and trust.

He came over to where I was seated and said, "I've got a present for you."

"What is it?" I asked excitedly.

"Close your eyes."

When I opened them, he was holding a cauliflower that comes packed in a pickle jar.

"I hid it from the kids," he said, "because I know how you like the cauliflower."

Maybe love was that simple.

A wedding anniversary is the celebration of

love, trust, partnership, tolerance, and

tenacity. The order varies for any given year.

PAUL SWEENEY

LETTERS HOME
FROM WAR

BY

BARBARA BARTOCCI

Tell me not, Sweet, I am unkind
That from the nunnery
Of thy chaste breast and quiet mind,
To war and arms I fly . . .
Yet this inconstancy is such
As you too shall adore;
I could not love thee, Dear, so much,
Loved I not honor more.

—RICHARD LOVELACE (1618–1657)

The style of war has changed since Lovelace's time, but the inner longings of the men who fight them have not. In 1967, Lieutenant Commander John E. Bartocci was on duty aboard the aircraft carrier Bon Homme Richard *(the* Bonnie Dick*) off the coast of Vietnam. He was a Navy fighter pilot, but also a husband and father. The warrior's passions, reflected in these excerpts from his letters to his family, are bound by no time or place.*

31 Jan. Dearest Barb, It was sad watching you and the children drive out of sight as the carrier pulled out of the harbor. Three years of shore duty were wonderful. The children's characters have really taken shape. I know them so much better now, and that makes leaving so much more difficult.

19 Feb. My birthday. Does thirty-three sound old? It used to, and I think it still does. When I went down to the Ready Room, I found a large birthday cake, and when I went up to man my aircraft, I found "Happy Birthday" written on the fuselage. We've got a good crew. I like them, and they know it.

Tomorrow is your birthday, but you don't age. You're as attractive as you were when you were seventeen years old—only now, more exciting. As I write these words, I'm thinking of you and how you act, sound, feel, smell. I'm so in love with you, Barb.

25 Feb. The time has come. Tomorrow we'll be on the line and I'm on the flight schedule. I feel like it was before an exam and I'm not prepared. Nervous as a cat. You can't imagine our schedule. My days start at 5:30 A.M. and go to 6:00 P.M. without a break. We then must share Condition I Air Defense (CAP) all night. (You sit in your aircraft ready to go. Two-hour watches per pilot.) Then we start again the next morning—for 28 days straight or until we leave the line. I admit I'm scared of the thought of getting shot at.

27 Feb. My first combat hop involved climbing through the clouds and heading for a target, only to find it was too far away. The problem then became one of landing back aboard in horrible weather. Windy, low ceilings.

A tragic loss today of one of our helicopters and crew. I played guitar with those pilots only last week.

5 March. You can't imagine what lousy weather we've been flying in. The men are fatigued and walking around in a daze.

I'm glad the children like my letters to them. I think it's better if they have a tangible communication from Daddy rather than just a word passed via you. I can just picture Andrew saying you "lost Daddy." Poor little guy. He can't know why the normal order of things is disturbed. I'm not sure I know, myself.

10 March. I'm back from a strike. It was a success. We (four planes) were the fighter cover and had to orbit inland to fend off MiGs if they came. No MiGs, but the 12 minutes we spent over North Vietnam seemed like ten years. My mouth was so dry. What a beautiful sight the sea is when you've crossed the coastline on the way back to the ship.

12 March. I'm sitting in the cockpit of an aircraft at 1:20 A.M. Condition I CAP. It's a lovely evening. The sea is calm and the only sound is the low whir of the gyros in my cockpit. Just now, I saw a falling star. It seems almost out of the question that I could go flying at a moment's notice.

I'm rambling on, Barb. Sort of mentally chatting with you. I can't think of anything substantial or joyous without thinking of you. I can't think of a most exquisite love without thinking of you.

16 March. By the time you get this letter you will undoubtedly have heard of the loss of Lieutenant j.g. Don S yesterday. Possibly he took an enemy hit, but visibility was poor. He may have just flown into the water. Don had been in the squadron a scant nine days.

23 April. Operations back to a steady pace. Fresh water is low. No showers allowed. After a sweaty day of flight ops, means lots of deodorant and aftershave lotion.

24 April. The dangers of this business hit home today. They bagged another of our squadron pilots. A parachute was seen so he is probably alive. I'm scheduled for a strike tomorrow. I shudder to think of capture. Please pray that I'll have the presence of mind to do my job properly and with honor.

3 May. Going on a big one again tomorrow. Things are hot out here now. It looks as if the war has escalated, but you probably have a better overall picture than we do.

Our airplanes aren't holding up at all, and we can't get parts. It's a frustrating business. My schedule has become disjointed. Up at 3:15 A.M. Fly two hops. Sleep at 2:00 P.M. Up at 5:00 P.M. Condition I CAP from ten till midnight. Up again at 6:00 A.M. And so it goes. And it's *hot.*

6 May. Waiting to go on a big strike the past two days but weather has prohibited. Still, life isn't boring—last night one of our aircraft caught fire on the flight deck. A sad note: this morning an enlisted man walked into a propeller. It was pretty messy. The damn flight deck continues to be a hazard, and the long hours don't help crew alertness. I hate accidents of that type. Here's a guy who is doing a difficult job—for peanuts—and putting up with long separations and lousy living conditions and he winds up dead.

After the pressures of this air war, I know what a treasure the serenity of the family is. I long to feel the children's arms around me, to play the role of the lion with his cubs. Tears come to my eyes when I think how I want to be with my children, playing with them, explaining things to them, trying to give them some of myself. And then to think of you, my greatest asset. You've flooded my life with goodness. You are the source of all that's dear to me.

14 May. We're now steaming full speed toward Yankee station, two days early. Could this be escalation? Stay tuned.

19 May. A bad day for us. The opposition was the worst ever, they say. Two pilots are reported missing. A good chance they were captured. I hope so. As one man put it yesterday, "You can't come back from the dead, but you might make it out of a prison camp."

20 May. I am scheduled for the next strike . . . a tough one . . . target is in downtown Hanoi. I don't mind telling you I'm scared. I hope I can get this out of my system prior to launch (I will, of course). By the time you receive this letter, the strike will be history.

21 May. I went to Mass this morning. We brief for the big strike at noon. Before the strike, Barb, it's important for me to tell you again how much I love you. Without you, my life would be shallow and empty.

. . . I am happy to be continuing this letter. The strike was a success and we got everyone back, which is the most important thing. I have done difficult things in my life but that has got to be the roughest. I had to fly right over downtown Hanoi. They shot everything in the book at us, and I'll bet I perspired five gallons of water.

31 May. Today was glorious in one way. Received a wonderful photograph of you and the children. Barb, I can't tell you not to worry or not to be afraid. All I can say is, I hope it's God's will that I return to you in August as scheduled. There is nothing I want more than to go on the camping trip that Barty keeps talking about.

2 June. Thanks for your letter with Barty's tooth in it! I wish I could hear Bart laugh right now. He has such an infectious laugh. I love him so. Tell Allison that I love my little girl very much. And Andrew, too.

3 June. I am sad to report that Dave W was lost at sea early this morning. Search is still in progress. He took off at 2:30 A.M., and that was the last contact. In the face of war, one tends to forget the hazards of flying off a carrier.

Hope you're saying some prayers. My emotions are a mix of self-pity, fear, pride, sadness, anger. I wonder if I have courage—and if I do, what is it all worth? Of course, we must maintain our outward appearance of fearless composure.

The supreme happiness of life is the conviction that we are loved.

VICTOR HUGO

4 June. We are inventorying and packing Dave's things. What a depressing job. I liked Dave better than anyone else in the squadron. I still can't get used to the idea he's gone.

P.S. Our flight surgeon just stopped in to give me a cigar. His wife gave birth to a girl. I told him, news of a *birth* is welcome, indeed.

6 June. Tomorrow I will have been commissioned for ten years, and next week we will have been married nine years. Nine wonderful years to a girl who makes me feel nine feet tall and who has borne me three beautiful children. Without you, my darling, I'd be like an autumn leaf—dry and lifeless. With you loving me, spring is always in the offing.

Again, sad news. Yesterday we lost a photo pilot. Just two days earlier, he and I had made the same run together. They were shooting like mad. Yesterday, they got lucky. Damn war. So depressing.

9 June. Dear Bart: How are you, son? I sure enjoyed the tape recording you, Mommy, Allison, and Andrew made. And I enjoyed your joke, too . . .

Dear Allison: I enjoy getting letters from you. Help your mother and be a good big sister to your brothers. Love, "Daddy-O"

12 June. A quiet Sunday. Only two big air strikes. John M got shot down east of Haiphong but was picked up. You can't imagine the anxiety of waiting for the Helo to get him. Alfred Hitchcock couldn't have duplicated the suspense. Yes sir, a drama a day.

A new pilot came aboard yesterday—an ensign. Poor kid was in the Ready Room when we got back from the Hanoi raid. Must have been something to see all these pilots come in soaked in their own perspiration, hair askew, with dry mouths, adrenalin still up and breathing heavy. That's a hell of a way to meet the squadron!

I'm looking at the beautiful pictures you sent me of the children. I see such *hope* in their eyes. I want so much to hold them in my arms, Barb. I want to be there to influence my children, to bring out their good qualities. What greater success can a father ask?

14 June. Awards were given out today, and I got my first air medal. The award that would please me would be a trip back home. Four more days of this line period. The ship expects to arrive in San Diego in August. That means our big camping trip is set for September.

27 June. Tomorrow starts our last line period. Thirty-two more days of combat . . . I want to hold you in my arms, taste the sweetness of your lips, feel the softness of your cheek next to mine, make love to you. How deeply I love you, darling.

3 July. Tomorrow is the Fourth of July. There's a theory that the North Viets are saving all their SAMs for tomorrow. I'm on the first launch. Three strikes a day until further notice. I don't think the idea of July Fourth has ever had so much meaning for me as it does now.

21 July. Big day for VF-24. Bob Kirkwood (my roommate) and Red Isaacks (XO) both shot down MiGs this morning. Good guys win, too.

25 July. Three more days till we leave the line.

29 July. I can't believe this has happened. This morning at 7:00 I was thinking happy thoughts. Combat flying was over. Bob and I congratulated each other on having conducted ourselves honorably and with excellence. At 11:00, we got word of a fire on the aircraft carrier *Forrestal*. We steamed full speed to give assistance. Smoke was billowing out of her stern section, and the charred remnants of some aircraft were visible on the flight deck. At least 20 people killed and a lot more injured.

How does it affect us? We're extended on the line for an indefinite period.

31 Aug.
My Darling John,

I love you. They're trying to tell me you're dead. You can't be—we have so much to do together. Remember our camping trip? Remember how we joke and laugh together?

Oh, John, I love you—John, you can't be dead . . .

Lieutenant Commander John Bartocci was killed when his aircraft crashed into the flight deck as he returned from a night mission. His body was lost at sea.

FIRST LOVE

BY
JOHN WALTERS

I remember the way the light touched her hair. She turned her head, and our eyes met, a momentary awareness in that raucous fifth-grade classroom. I felt as though I'd been struck a blow under the heart. Thus began my first love affair.

Her name was Rachel, and I mooned my way through grade and high school, stricken at the mere sight of her, tongue-tied in her presence. Does anyone, anymore, linger in the shadows of evening, drawn by the pale light of a window—*her* window—like some hapless summer insect? That delirious swooning, asexual but urgent and obsessive, that made me awkward and my voice crack, is like some impossible dream now. I know I was so afflicted, but I cannot actually believe what memory insists I did. Which was to suffer. Exquisitely.

I would catch sight of her, walking down an aisle of trees to or from school, and I'd become paralyzed. She always seemed so poised, so self-possessed. At home, I'd relive each encounter, writhing at the thought of my inadequacies. Even so, as we entered our teens, I sensed her affectionate tolerance for me.

"Going steady" implied a maturity we still lacked. Her Orthodox Jewish upbringing and my own Catholic scruples imposed a celibate grace that made even kissing a distant prospect, however fervently desired. I managed to hold her once at a dance—chaperoned, of course. Our embrace made her giggle, a sound so trusting that I hated myself for what I'd been thinking.

At any rate, my love for Rachel remained unrequited. We graduated from high school, she went on to college, and I joined the Army. When World War II engulfed us, I was sent overseas. For a time we corresponded, and her letters were the highlight of those grinding, endless years. Once she sent me a snapshot of herself in a bathing suit, which drove me to the wildest of fantasies. I mentioned the possibility of marriage in my next letter, and almost immediately her replies became less frequent, less personal.

The first thing I did when I returned to the States was to call on Rachel. Her mother answered the door. Rachel no longer lived there. She had married a medical student she'd met in college. "I thought she wrote you," her mother said.

Her "Dear John" letter finally caught up with me while I was awaiting discharge. She gently explained the impossibility of a marriage between us. Looking back on it, I must have recovered rather quickly, although for the first few months I believed I didn't want to live. Like Rachel, I found someone else, whom I learned to love with a deep and permanent commitment that has lasted to this day.

Then, recently, after an interval of more than 40 years, I heard from Rachel again. Her husband had died. She was passing through town and had learned of my whereabouts through a mutual friend. We agreed to meet.

I felt both curious and excited. In the last few years, I hadn't thought about her, and her sudden call one morning had taken me aback. The actual sight of her was a shock. This white-haired matron at the

restaurant table was the Rachel of my dreams and desires, the supple mermaid of that snapshot?

Yet time had given us a common reference and respect. We talked as old friends, and quickly discovered we were both grandparents.

"Do you remember this?" She handed me a slip of worn paper. It was a poem I'd written her while still in school. I examined the crude meter and pallid rhymes. Watching my face, she snatched the poem from me and returned it to her purse, as though fearful I was going to destroy it.

I told her about the snapshot, how I'd carried it all through the war.

"It wouldn't have worked out, you know," she said.

"How can you be sure?" I countered. "Ah, colleen, it might have been grand indeed—my Irish conscience and your Jewish guilt!"

Our laughter startled people at a nearby table. During the time left to us, our glances were furtive, oblique. I think that what we saw in each other repudiated what we'd once been to ourselves, we immortals.

Before I put her into a taxi, she turned to me. "I just wanted to see you once more. To tell you something." Her eyes met mine. "I wanted to thank you for having loved me as you did." We kissed, and she left.

From a store window my reflection stared back at me, an aging man with gray hair stirred by an evening breeze. I decided to walk home. Her kiss still burned on my lips. I felt faint, and sat on a park bench. All around me the grass and trees were shining in the surreal glow of sunset. Something was being lifted out of me. Something had been completed, and the scene before me was so beautiful that I wanted to shout and dance and sing for joy.

That soon passed, as everything must, and presently I was able to stand and start for home.

Chains do not hold a marriage together. It

is threads, hundreds of tiny threads, which

sew people together through the years.

SIMONE SIGNORET

"EMMA, I WON'T LEAVE YOU"

BY
EMILY AND PER OLA D'AULAIRE

It was a sunny February morning in Southern California, and Larry Shannon and his wife, Emma, were in high spirits. They had been on the road in their 22-foot motor home for almost four months, had visited a daughter in Florida, and would soon arrive at the home of another daughter, Patti, in Modesto. There they planned to spend several months before heading back home to Michigan.

Larry had celebrated his eighty-second birthday just the day before, and Emma was two years younger. They had been married 52 years. After their six children were grown, Larry retired from his trade as a master welder, and the couple took to traveling around the country. Then Emma's health began to fail—now she was a semi-invalid. Larry devoted himself to nursing her and keeping her spirits up.

One day in 1974, as they were talking in their Grand Rapids home, Larry suddenly grew serious. "Emma," he said, "we're not going to sit around here waiting to see which one of us calls the undertaker first. We're going to get a motor home and really see this country."

A vigorous, wiry Irishman with bright blue eyes, snowy white hair, and neatly trimmed mustache, Larry Shannon was not easily dissuaded once he made up his mind. "We'll keep off the freeways and travel on country roads," he told Emma. "That way we won't have to drive so fast, and we'll see more."

Driving now in the southern foothills of the High Sierra, Larry pulled over and looked at his road map. "We'll take that route," he said, pointing to a thin blue line that snaked through the mountains and came down in the fertile San Joaquin Valley.

The road he had chosen starts out along the raging Kern River, then climbs steeply westward to cross a 6400-foot pass before dropping to California's central valley. About noon, Larry began to worry. It had clouded up and started to snow, and there were not many places along the narrow mountain road in which to turn a motor home around. He glanced at his map. "The next town should be just down the road," he said. "We'll wait out the storm there."

What Larry Shannon didn't know was that he was on the wrong road. With the center line hidden under snow, he had blundered off the correct route onto a Forest Service side road, unmaintained in winter. Ahead, the road came to a dead end at a deserted boys' camp, and beyond that lay some of the most rugged wilderness in the United States.

It was 1:00 P.M. when they got stuck. As Larry slowed for a sharp curve, the rear wheels broke through an underlying crust of old snow and began to spin. Wrapped in a sweater and two coats, he got out to survey the situation. The narrow road was practically hewn into the side of a cliff. On his left, needle-sharp 8000-foot peaks towered 2500 feet above him; on his right was a 1000-foot drop-off into a canyon.

The Shannons had been traveling through southern states and had no shovel, chains, or even boots. Using a three-quart saucepan as a scoop, Larry worked unsuccessfully for two hours to clear the snow from the rear wheels. Finally, cold and wet, he heeded Emma's pleas that he come inside. "I'll get us out tomorrow," he promised her. It was Tuesday, February 7, 1978.

About 2:00 A.M. Wednesday, the Shannons heard a rumbling that shook the motor home and set their toy poodle, Andy, to barking. At daylight, they saw that a rockslide had cascaded down the mountain, piling several tons of debris on the road ahead. It had stopped snowing. But if another slide were to hit their vehicle, Larry realized, they'd be crushed or swept into the canyon below. Urgently, he switched on the CB radio and spent most of the day trying to contact a sheriff's department, a ranger station . . . anyone. Hemmed in by high peaks, his signal was never heard. By 2:00 P.M. he felt it was useless, but he showed Emma how to work the CB before turning his attention to the motor home.

With a tire iron he chipped away at some ice where the wheels had dug in, then started the engine and worked the vehicle free. Just as he began to move forward, however, there was a sudden lurch, followed by a snapping sound. The universal joint had broken. "Well," he told Emma, trying to sound cheerful, "we'll just have to sit it out until somebody picks us up." At 5:00 P.M. it started to snow again.

It snowed all day Thursday, while Larry kept up a steady stream of conversation to buoy Emma's spirits. "We've got one thing in our favor," he told her. "When we don't show up, Patti will get worried and call the police." Larry toasted all their bread on the gas stove so it wouldn't mold, and then surveyed the canned-food supply. "We've got plenty to eat," he said. "We'll be okay." They played cards, talked about their six children, laughed about the past. And tried to forget the present.

Around four the following afternoon, Larry was helping Emma out of her seat when she went limp. He thought it was one of her fainting spells, but as he leaned over her, he was suddenly overcome himself by the dizziness and nausea of altitude sickness. He barely made it to the bunk before passing out. When he woke it was dark. He fumbled for a light and found Emma on the floor, breathing heavily. Too weak to move her, he put a pillow under her head, covered her with a blanket, and collapsed back on the bunk.

At 3:00 A.M., Larry was awakened by a whining, near-frantic Andy. He went over to Emma. She wasn't breathing. He reached for her hand. It was cold; there was no pulse. Emma was dead.

Dazed, he closed her eyes, then knelt and prayed. *When they find us next spring,* he thought, *they'll likely find me beside her. Well, we came through life together—and we'll end it together.*

In the morning, however, Larry's will to live was rekindled by a fierce determination to take care of Emma to the last. Afraid that animals would get at her body if he put her out in the snow, he covered her with blankets and an overcoat, laid her on the floor where it was coolest, and turned off the propane furnace. *Emma,* he vowed, *I won't leave you.* And then Larry Shannon set about the business of survival.

When her parents didn't show up by the weekend, Patti Spurr began to worry. Nasty weather throughout Southern California had unleashed a rash of mudslides. Could their motor home have been buried under an avalanche? Police in the area assured her that all mudslides had been systematically checked out. No green-and-white motor home with Michigan plates had been spotted.

She called the highway patrol but was told they couldn't help unless they had some idea where to look. "If there are a hundred and three ways to go, Dad will take the hundred and fourth," Patti says. "I didn't know what to tell them."

Larry watched the snow mount until it reached a height of six feet. Several times a day he pushed the door open to keep it from being blocked, then shoveled the snow away with a saucepan. He ticked the days off on a calendar, kept a careful log of both inside and outside temperatures, and wrote his thoughts in a notebook. Inside, the mercury dipped to 20 degrees at night. He donned two sets of insulated underwear, two sweaters, and two pairs of socks to keep warm.

The weather let up briefly that first Sunday, and Larry watched as five deer climbed up from the canyon, only their heads and necks visible above the deep powder. Then it began to snow again. It didn't slacken until February 14, a week after the ordeal had begun.

Larry woke up that morning full of hope. The sun was shining and the snow "glittered like diamonds." He pushed open the door, then began shoveling a path around the motor home with the saucepan and clearing off the roof to make it more visible from the air. He heard the sound of a jet overhead, and dashed inside for emergency flares. But by then it was gone. He spent the rest of the day working the CB—without success—and once more his spirits fell. *It's a hell of a way to end 82 years,* he thought. *But if that's it, that's it.*

Yet, somehow, Larry's will to survive won out again. He continued clearing off the roof and shoveling a path so he and Andy could exercise. He melted snow on the propane stove for drinking water, and forced himself to eat two meals a day to maintain his strength. The Shannons had stocked up on citrus a few days before getting stuck. Now Larry ate half a grapefruit every morning, along with a piece of the toasted bread. For dinner, he drew on the motor home's supply of canned soups and preserves.

In Modesto, Patti Spurr and her husband, George, stepped up their efforts. On the off chance that her parents had been delayed and simply forgotten to phone her, Patti asked a nearby TV station to flash a message on the screen requesting them to call. When the

> *A happy marriage is a long conversation that always seems too short.*
>
> ANDRÉ MAUROIS

152

Spurrs contacted the Civil Air Patrol, they were told that a statewide aerial survey had already been carried out. No vehicle like the Shannons' had been found.

For Larry Shannon, things looked grim. Clouds had rolled in over the mountains; for five days heavy rain pelted the metal roof. On March 7, the twenty-ninth day, the weather cleared and an Air Force jet shot low through the canyon to the right, almost at eye-level, rattling the windows of the motor home. It made three passes, circling around to the south, then roaring back up the canyon—and Larry thought he saw a signal light flash from the cockpit.

He was so excited he didn't sleep a wink that night. He turned on the cabin lights for the first time since Emma's death (to save the battery, he hadn't used them), shaved, and packed a bag, expecting to be evacuated. But the following day nothing happened. The "signal" had been a cruel deception, a sun reflection on the plane's metal skin. "It's hard to get your hopes up and be let down," he recorded. "But that's life, I guess."

On the morning of March 10, Larry was marking off the thirty-second day on his calendar when a sudden chattering noise brought him scrambling outside just in time to see a helicopter's tail rotor disappear around the mountainside. The three men in the chopper—bound for a check of the boys' camp at the end of the service road—stared in disbelief. They circled back, and this time saw a white-haired man in a red-plaid shirt waving his arms at them.

With a bare six feet between the whirling blades and the side of the granite wall, pilot Bob Wasik set down the chopper, rocking it into the snow for stability. While the blades were still whirring, the three men leaped from the craft and waded through the wet snow toward Larry. The first man to reach him, John Bethell, embraced him in a bear hug.

"You're an angel from heaven," Larry Shannon said in a thin voice. And then, for the first time since his 32-day ordeal began, he wept.

Funeral services for Emma Shannon were held in Modesto a few days after the rescue. On Easter Sunday, Larry returned to the motor home accompanied by a grandson-in-law and his friend. They replaced the universal joint; then the young men watched amazed as Larry maneuvered the vehicle around the rockslide, and out of the mountains. Although he had lost 16 pounds, Larry was otherwise in good health. His zest for life undimmed, he soon announced plans to drive the motor home back to Grand Rapids.

Bob McAdams, the third member of the rescue group, summed it all up: "Larry Shannon is an example of the indomitable spirit of man. He just wouldn't give up."

"Mother's spirit was also involved," adds Patti. "If Dad had tried to walk out alone, he would have perished. So even in death, Mother took care of him. She saved his life, because he wouldn't leave her there."

Love is perhaps the only glimpse we are
permitted of eternity.

HELEN HAYES

AN IRISH LOVE STORY

BY

GEORGE TARGET

Let's call him Ian. That's not his real name—but in Northern Ireland these days you have to be careful about revealing names. There have been more than 2400 sectarian murders since the recent flare-up of ancient troubles between Catholics and Protestants. So there's no sense taking risks.

And Ian has had misery enough for his twenty-four years of life.

He came from good Protestant stock, the sort that goes to church twice every Sunday as regular as clockwork. His father, a welder in the Belfast shipyards, steady as they come. Mother kept a clean and tidy house, baked the best bread in the neighborhood, and ruled the family with the sharp edge of her tongue. Two elder brothers, both unemployed laborers.

Ian did well at school and was now earning good money as a craftsman in a production plant. Quiet, serious, fond of walking through the countryside during the green evenings and golden weekends of summer, he liked few things better than a book by the roaring fire during the long loneliness of winter. Never had much to do with girlfriends—though men tend to marry late in Ireland.

Two years earlier, on his twenty-second birthday, he was walking home from work when a terrorist hurled a bomb from a speeding car . . . and left Ian babbling in the nightmare of sudden blindness.

He was rushed to a hospital, operated on immediately for internal injuries and broken bones. But both eyes were destroyed.

The other wounds healed in their own time, though their scars would disfigure his flesh the rest of his days. But the scars on his mind, though invisible, were even more obvious.

He hardly spoke a word, hardly ate or drank, hardly slept. He simply lay in bed, brooding and sightless. Nearly four months.

There was one nurse who seemed to be able to draw some small spark of human response from him.

Let's call her Bridget—a fine Irish name. Good Catholic stock, the sort that goes to Mass first thing every Sunday morning.

Her father, a carpenter, mostly worked away from home over in England. A decent man—loved his family, spent weekends with them whenever he could afford the fare. And they loved him as only an absent father can be loved.

Mother kept a clean but untidy house, cooked the best stew in the neighborhood, and ruled the family with a quick hand and a soft heart.

Six brothers, four sisters—with the youngest of them all, Mary, eleven, her father's darling.

Bridget did well at school, had trained as a nurse at a famous London hospital, and now, at the age of twenty-one, was a staff nurse in Belfast's biggest hospital.

Lively, though fundamentally serious, a singer with a sweet and gentle voice and a way of her own with folk songs. Never had much to do with boyfriends—though it wasn't from any lack of young men who'd set their caps at her.

But now her heart was moved by Ian, for there was something of the little-boy-lost about him that brought tears to her eyes. True, he couldn't see the tears, yet she was afraid that her voice would betray her emotions.

In a way she was right about her voice, because it was the lilt and the laughter of it that dragged him back from the depths of depression and self-pity, the warmth and gentleness and strength of her words, the blessed assurance with which she spoke to him of the love of Jesus Christ.

And so, as the long dark of his days turned to weeks and months, he would listen for her footsteps and turn his sightless face toward her coming like a flower bending for the sun.

At the end of his four months in the hospital he was pronounced incurably blind, but what he now knew as their love gave him the courage to accept his affliction. Because, despite everything against them— religion, politics, the opposition of their families—they were in love, and wandering in that young and singing landscape.

He was discharged and began the weary months of rehabilitation: how to wash and shave and dress without help, how to move around the house without cracking his shins on every chair, how to walk through the streets with a white stick, how to read Braille, how to survive the crushing pity he could sense in the very air he breathed. Their love gave him the hope to go on living and trying.

Not that they were able to spend much of their lives together: an occasional evening, perhaps an afternoon when her duties allowed. But they lived for those brief encounters and knew the beginnings of deep peace and high joys.

Their families were appalled. Thinking of getting married? The very law of God forbade it, surely.

"What fellowship hath the children of light with the children of darkness?" thundered his father. "You'll not be marrying her whilst I'm drawing breath!"

"The Roman Catholic Church," stated her priest, "discourages mixed marriages, so you can be putting the idea from you!"

So, by all manner of pressures—constant arguments, threats, promises, and even downright lies—they were driven apart. And, eventually, they quarreled, said hurtful things in their black misery, and one evening, with the rain drizzling and their hearts cold, she walked away from him on the weeping street.

He withdrew into his perpetual night. Days and weeks of bitterness. "You'll not be regretting it in the long run," he was told. "You'd have been inviting trouble by yoking with an unbeliever!"

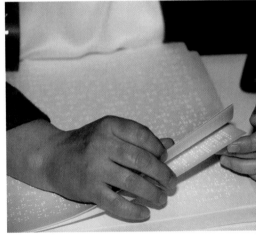

She withdrew into her work, too sick at heart to remember. Weeks and months of numbed agony. "You'll live to praise the Almighty," she was told. "You'd have been asking for hell on earth marrying a Protestant!"

The months drained into a year. And the bombings continued, to the grief of Ireland.

Then one evening, as Ian sat alone in the house, there came a frantic hammering at the door. "Ian! Come you quick!"

By the voice, hysterical, choked with tears, he recognized young Mary, Bridget's sister. "A bombing! She's trapped and half-dead, so she is! Screaming after you. Come you, Ian! In the name of God, please come!"

Without even shutting the door behind him, he took her hand. And she led and stumbled and cried with him through the merciless streets.

The bomb had devastated a little restaurant where Bridget had been eating supper with three other nurses. The others had managed to scramble out from under the shifting rubble. But she was trapped by the legs. And the fire was spreading, licking toward her.

They could hear her screaming, but couldn't yet reach the pit where she lay. Firemen, soldiers, lights, and special equipment were on their way.

Ian moved into the chaos. "You can't go in there!" shouted the officer in charge.

"She's my girl," said Ian.

"Don't be a raving lunatic!" shouted the officer. "You'll not be seeing your hand in front of your face in the darkness!"

"What difference does darkness make to a blind man?" said Ian.

And he turned toward the sound of her voice, and moved through that black inferno with all the skills and instincts of the blind, all the urgency of love. "I'm coming, Bridget! I'm coming!"

And he found her, and cradled her head in his yearning arms, and kissed her.

"Ian," she whispered, "Ian . . ." and lapsed into unconsciousness like a tired child.

And with her blood soaking into his clothes, the fire reaching them, he held her until their rescuers chopped a way through. What he didn't see, being blind, was that the side of her lovely face had been seared by fire.

In time, a long time, she recovered. Despite cosmetic surgery, though, her face would always be scarred. "But," she said, "the only man I love will never have the seeing of it, so what difference does it make to me?" And they took up their love from where they had never really left it.

True, both families resisted every step of the way. One dramatic confrontation almost led to a fistfight: shouted abuse, insults, desperate

The course of true love never did run smooth.

WILLIAM SHAKESPEARE

threats. But, in the middle of it, Bridget took Ian's hand. And together they walked out of that place of hatred.

Yes, they would marry. All the conventional wisdom warns of failure. But do you know a more excellent way than love? And what other healing is there?

Marriage resembles a pair of shears, so joined
that they cannot be separated; often moving
in opposite directions, yet always punishing
anyone who comes between them.

SYDNEY SMITH

A STORY FOR VALENTINE'S DAY

BY

JO ANN LARSEN

Larry and Jo Ann were an ordinary couple. They lived in an ordinary house on an ordinary street. Like other ordinary couples, they struggled to make ends meet and to do the right things for their children.

They were ordinary in yet another way—they had their squabbles. Much of their conversation concerned what was wrong in their marriage and who was to blame.

Until one day, when a most extraordinary event took place.

"You know, Jo Ann, I've got a magic chest of drawers. Every time I open them, they're full of socks and underwear," Larry said. "I want to thank you for filling them all these years."

Jo Ann stared at her husband over the top of her spectacles. "What do you want, Larry?"

"Nothing. I just want you to know I appreciate those magic drawers."

This wasn't the first time Larry had done something odd, so Jo Ann pushed the incident out of her mind until a few days later.

164

"Jo Ann, thank you for recording so many correct check numbers in the ledger this month. You put down the right number fifteen out of sixteen times. That's a record."

Disbelieving what she had heard, Jo Ann looked up from her mending: "Larry, you're always complaining about my recording the wrong check numbers. Why stop now?"

"No reason. I just wanted you to know I appreciate the effort you're making."

Jo Ann shook her head and went back to her mending. "What's gotten into him?" she mumbled.

Nevertheless, the next day when Jo Ann wrote a check at the grocery store, she glanced at her checkbook to confirm that she had put down the right check number. *Why do I suddenly care about those dumb check numbers?* she asked herself.

She tried to disregard the incident, but Larry's strange behavior intensified.

"Jo Ann, that was a great dinner," he said one evening. "I appreciate all your effort. Why, in the past fifteen years I'll bet you've fixed over 14,000 meals for me and the kids."

Then "Gee, Jo Ann, the house looks spiffy. You've really worked hard to get it looking so good." And even "Thanks, Jo Ann, for just being you. I really enjoy your company."

Jo Ann was growing worried. *Where's the sarcasm, the criticism?* she wondered.

Her fears that something peculiar was happening to her husband were confirmed by sixteen-year-old Shelly, who complained, "Dad's gone bonkers, Mom. He just told me I looked nice. With all this makeup and these sloppy clothes, he still said it. That's not Dad, Mom. What's wrong with him?"

Whatever was wrong, Larry didn't get over it. Day in and day out he continued focusing on the positive. Over the weeks, Jo Ann grew

more used to her mate's unusual behavior, and occasionally even gave him a grudging "thank you." She prided herself in taking it all in stride, until one day something so peculiar happened she became completely discombobulated:

"I want you to take a break," Larry said. "I am going to do the dishes. So please take your hands off that frying pan and leave the kitchen."

(Long, long pause.) "Thank you, Larry. Thank you very much!"

Jo Ann's step was now a little lighter, her self-confidence higher, and once in a while she hummed. She didn't seem to experience blue moods much anymore. *I rather like Larry's new behavior,* she thought.

That would be the end of the story except one day, another most extraordinary event took place. This time it was Jo Ann who spoke.

"Larry," she said, "I want to thank you for going to work and providing for us all these years. I don't think I've ever told you how much I appreciate it."

Larry has never revealed the reason for his dramatic change of behavior no matter how hard Jo Ann has pushed for an answer, and so it will likely remain one of life's mysteries. But it's one I'm thankful to live with.

You see, I am Jo Ann.

We come to love not by finding a perfect

person but by learning to see an imperfect

person perfectly.

SAM KEEN

"I WISH I COULD HOLD YOU MORE"

BY

BONNIE REMSBERG

August 11, 1986, was a busy day at the Wagner household in suburban Chicago. Brett, twenty-five, was in the backyard cutting the grass. Five-year-old Brent was "helping" his father. Blair, Brett's three-year-old daughter, and Blaine, his two-year-old son, were splashing in a little plastic pool. Debbie Wagner was in the kitchen, cutting curtains for her daughter's room. Suddenly Brent burst in. "Mommy!" he screamed. "Daddy's shaking and turning blue!"

Debbie raced outside and found Brett thrashing on the ground. Running back into the house, she dialed 911 for an ambulance. Paramedics arrived moments later, and Brett was rushed to Alexian Brothers Medical Center in Elk Grove Village, Illinois.

Over the next week, a number of tests were taken, including a CAT scan. The doctor who gave the results to Debbie was pale. "Mrs. Wagner," he said, "I'm sorry." Brett had a tumor pressing on his brain and others in a lung. Her husband had only a few months to live.

Brett insisted on going home to be with his family. It would not be easy, but with the added help of the Alexian Brothers hospice team, and that of friends, it was possible.

Brett's tumors grew rapidly, affecting his balance, emotions, and short-term memory. But he was determined to leave behind a testament of his love for his family, a little bit of himself for Debbie and the children to hold on to. Over the next several months, Brett marshaled the strength to record his thoughts on videotape. Speaking sometimes through tears, sometimes with laughter, he recorded glimpses of himself, myriad little details—shoe size, favorite cars, attitudes about work—"the kinds of things," says Debbie, "that get lost with time."

Brett made four tapes in all, telling his children that "this will let you know a little about me, how I feel about things that are important." He sat at a table in front of the camera, dressed in a sport shirt, sipping a soft drink. Sometimes he looked down at notes he had made. In the later tapes the pressure of the brain tumor, the strain, and the medication had taken their toll. He tired quickly. Still, he talked on.

Brent, Blair, Blaine. I want you to be able to understand what happened. I know it will be hard. I'm twenty-five, and I can't accept a lot of this myself.

Sometimes I feel as if we all got robbed, but certain things can't be changed, and we have to accept that.

Just don't ever give up. Try to be concerned about other people's feelings. You should always care, because there are people you can trust and believe in. Your mother is one.

Brett and Debbie were only fifteen years old when they met at Schaumburg High School. She was pretty, with wide green eyes. She first saw Brett walking another girl to class. He was muscular and broad-shouldered, with an infectious smile and curly hair. "Who is that?" she asked a friend. "I want to get to know him."

Debbie recalls the exact moment of their first kiss, on April Fools' Day, at ten to eleven in the morning in the downstairs hallway at Schaumburg. *I'm going to marry this guy,* she said to herself afterward. Soon, they were inseparable.

Debbie and I have been together so much you can probably count on your two hands the times that we were separated. But the first time I realized I was in love was during one of our fights. We told each other, "Oh, forget it. We're not going to stay together." But when I left, I felt something in my chest, and I just knew I loved her.

Brett was the kind of kid who tinkered—lawn mowers, bicycles, anything he could get his hands on. He began working at age twelve and always had some kind of job. In high school, he worked afternoons and weekends for his father, Gil, an auto mechanic. After graduation, he worked with his father full time.

In 1978, Debbie graduated and became a cashier at a neighborhood supermarket. She saved her money to buy Brett his first tool kit. Just before Christmas, he proposed, on one knee, as she sat at his mother's kitchen table.

Most of their relatives told them they were crazy—they were too young, they had no money, they had dated only one another. The pastor of Saint Peter Lutheran Church gave them a marriage compatibility test, which they felt they failed. In the car on the way home, Debbie cried and Brett laughed.

On November 30, 1979, in a candlelight service, Debbie and Brett were married. Each had just turned nineteen years old, and they couldn't afford a honeymoon.

We did a fair amount of fighting in our early days. That's something everybody does. But you have to work out the bugs. Marriage is almost like getting along with your brothers or your sister. You've got to give a little, and they've got to give a little. I always loved giving to your mother.

Brett and Debbie's social life consisted of television, pizza in the living room, an occasional movie. Brett was content. Then, two weeks before their first anniversary, Debbie took a home-pregnancy test and, gleeful, left the results on a counter for Brett to find. "The nurturing instinct was born into that man," Debbie says. "Oh, did he want that baby."

Brent, I was there to watch you being born. I was so nervous. That's part of being human. You're going to be nervous about things. You're going to be scared. I want you not to worry, because everything will work out.

Brent was born in August of 1981. Blair came along less than two years later. The family barely scraped by on Brett's commissions from repair work and Debbie's part-time income from the supermarket.

In October, a few months after their daughter was born, Brett had a vasectomy. The next week, Debbie learned that she was expecting again.

Blaine, you're special. You kind of snuck in there. And just like your brother and sister, you were made with love. That's what matters.

As far as taking care of you guys—changing diapers and fixing bottles—I did the night shift a lot. You're half my responsibility, because you're half of me. You're all so much like me. Your mom always said, "They all look like you. How come?" Well, she's going to see me every morning when you wake up.

There were good times and bad after Blaine was born, busy times. Debbie and Brett were still pressed for money, but they were happy.

Then, in March 1985, Gil Wagner noticed that a facial mole Brett had had since childhood looked different. "You'd better have a doctor look at that," he told his son.

A plastic surgeon removed the mole, the size of a pencil eraser. A routine biopsy found it to be a malignant melanoma.

A week later, Brett went into the hospital, where doctors removed some lymph nodes, small veins, and an egg-size piece of flesh around the mole. Test results, the doctor told Debbie and Brett on follow-up visits, were negative.

When Brett recovered, he went back to work. Shortly thereafter, his dad decided to close the business, and Brett decided to open his own.

> *There is no fear in love; but perfect love casteth out fear.*
>
> I JOHN 4

I never really had much of a strategy after high school. Following in my dad's footsteps, I ended up being a mechanic. I've been working on cars for seven and a half years. It's in my blood. Without those tools in my kit there would be no bread on our table. I want my tools to go to Brent and Blaine. They will remind you of me.

Don't think your dad wants you to be a mechanic. The most important thing is to work at something you enjoy, and to always do it right.

Brett rented an unheated garage behind a house. He worked hard and was reliable, and several businesses started recommending him. Satisfied customers told others.

Several months after Brett rented the garage, the house in front became available, and he decided to rent it and move the family in. Now he could spend more time with Debbie and the kids.

It was 11 days after they moved in that Brett had his seizure.

Your mother is going to need your hugs. Brent, you can help her the most, because you're the oldest. You're real smart. I want you to keep learning and growing and to help your brother and sister. You're a big guy. You may not realize it, but you are.

Blair, I looked at some pictures of you this morning, and you're a cutie-pie, so free and independent. You have always had a lot of joy in you. Keep that happiness.

Blaine, you're so small, everyone might try to push you around, but I know you're going to be yourself. You're a good little guy.

The longest tape and the most difficult was the one Debbie and Brett made together. Debbie, fighting tears, sat beside him and asked questions. What's your favorite magazine? What jobs do you like to do around the house? They faced the camera; under the table their feet were entwined. They talked for almost two hours. At the end, fatigue was evident on their faces.

I don't mind vacuuming or doing the dishes. I have to be kind of in the mood, though. I'm really not a gung-ho cleaning person like your mother. She's always kept the house real sharp.

Don't ever forget that your mother has always been a good partner and a good wife. She's been right there with me. And I want you guys to help her out as much as you can. Just remember that I love you.

In mid-October, with money from a trust fund started for the family, Brett and Debbie, who had never been away together, managed to go to Hawaii on a belated honeymoon. They ate pizza on the beach at sunset. They swam and made love. Brett rented a Jet Ski, took it out, and saw a giant sea turtle. "It was fantastic," he told Debbie.

But on the plane coming home, he had another seizure. He was in the hospital for a week.

On Halloween, he and Debbie took their children out trick-or-treating. Four days later he was back in the hospital. His deterioration was steady; but he still wanted to be with his family. "When am I going to go home?" he kept asking. "I want to go home."

Debbie fought aggressively, and after three weeks she convinced the staff that she could administer the necessary medication and care for him with Gil's help. So Brett went home.

My favorite time of year is probably autumn because everything is changing. My favorite holiday? I'd say Thanksgiving, because of the turkey and the family being together. A big sit-down dinner. That's what I like.

Debbie cooked for the entire family on Thanksgiving, but Brett was semicomatose. November 30 was their seventh wedding anniversary. He pressed hard to rally, to talk with the kids, to keep connected, but he was slipping away.

By the tenth of December, Brett was exhausted from the fight. Everyone, including Brett, knew it was almost over. Gil was there, and Brent and Debbie and their friend Bill.

"We're here. Don't be afraid," Debbie said, laying her head on Brett's chest. "Good-bye, my love," she whispered. "Go to God. We love you."

I know you're fighters. I'm going to be watching over you, because I do believe there is a God. I want you to know that I'll be somewhere, still thinking about you and loving you and waiting for you.

Deb, the time has gone by so fast. I'm sorry it's got to be this way. I want you to be brave.

I don't ever want to say good-bye, ever. And I don't think I'm going to. Because I'm going to see you again.

Brent, Blair, Blaine. When you feel like you should be holding me, hold your mother. It will be like you're hugging me, because she's half of me.

I just wish I could hold you more.

Love is the final end of the world's history,

the Amen of the Universe.

NOVALIS

A swan sometimes thinks a member of another species is its mother or mate.

SEASON OF THE SWAN

BY

MARGOT MCWILLIAMS

The strange black bird drifted into the harbor on a westerly wind and an incoming tide. On that July 4, 1992, the handful of families of Matinicus Island, a speck of rock far off the coast of Maine, were having a cookout on the beach when the children saw her. When they offered hot-dog and hamburger rolls, the bird swam close and ate hungrily.

This starved, dehydrated, bedraggled clump of feathers with a long, arching neck was a swan. Despite a right wing that had been cut off at its midpoint, she had the air of a princess who had somehow misplaced her crown.

Incapable of flight, she had swum across at least 23 miles of ocean. If the winds and tides had been just a bit different, she would have been carried into the open Atlantic, to certain death.

Finally she gathered her strength, waddled onto the beach, and allowed lobsterman Mark Bemis to pick her up, put her in the back of his pickup, and deliver her to the bustling poultry yard of my next-door neighbor Elaine. As soon as the swan was put down, she spied the

176

freshwater pond at the edge of the woods and, dipping her beak, drank long and hard.

Within days, she recovered her strength and held sway over the whole island—her importance marked by the many arguments about her name. "Ruby Lips," Mark said, referring to her brilliant pouting red beak.

"Mariah," Elaine proclaimed, "because the wind blew her in." Mariah won out.

Mariah had thick black feathers with a dazzling underlayer of white, which she spent a lot of time fluffing about, like a chorus girl before the curtain goes up. Even her conversation was seductive. "Hee-hoo" she would repeat in a delicate soprano.

No one had seen a bird like this before. Elaine and I called Jody Jones, a wildlife biologist at the Maine Audubon Society. "Sounds like an Australian black swan," she said. "They're not native to the United States, but some people keep them as pets."

"Swans mate for life," Jody added. "The chances are that her mate has been killed. When that happens, the surviving spouse abandons the nest to seek another mate."

Two weeks later, Elaine received a phone call from a woman on Islesboro, an island 30 miles away. She had heard about the black swan.

"My husband and I owned a pair," she told Elaine. "They had their wings pinioned so they wouldn't fly away." But this made them vulnerable to predators, and the male was killed by a fox. Soon afterward, the female vanished. "We bought a new pair," she said. "You can keep her."

Now we looked at Mariah with new respect. Unable to take to the skies to follow her instinct, she had let the currents carry her where they would. Needing fresh water to survive, she had endured 30 miles of salt before finding safe harbor.

I asked Jody about another Australian black swan for a mate, but Mariah had already found what she was looking for.

My fiancé Arbus Ames and I had met eight years before. With a weathered face and arms strong from hauling 300 lobster traps a day into his boat, he seemed as solid as the granite coast. A divorced mother of four, I had promised to join Arbus on Matinicus when my youngest daughter went off to college. If I could adapt to life on an island with a population of only 40 people, we would marry. Now that my nest was finally empty, I was settling in, only to find myself competing with another empty nester. Mariah was as partial to Arbus as I was.

At first, she played hard to get. For days, Arbus sat on Elaine's porch, holding out bread. Mariah ignored him. When he admitted defeat and stood up to leave, she would, as if on cue, mince her way toward him.

Then it was his stubborn turn. Arbus wouldn't toss the bread. If Mariah wanted it, she would have to take it from his hand. He spent days at this game, and in the end she extended that long neck and delicately extricated a crust from his fingers. The bird was hooked.

One morning a week later I was awakened by a cross between a scream for help and a war whoop. It was 6:00 A.M., and I could hear Arbus in his truck rattling down the dirt road to the shore. When I looked out the window, I saw Mariah gazing toward Arbus's retreating truck.

I thought nothing of it until four that afternoon, when the hair-raising screech pierced the air again. Mariah was in the road, trumpeting and waiting for Arbus.

Up the road came Arbus's truck. He stopped under the big spruce tree in front of our home. Grinning broadly, he got out and said, "Hi ya, sweetie!"—to Mariah. Thus was born a twice-daily ritual of passionate farewells, noisy welcome homes, and an affair that had the whole island talking.

On the water, by radio, fellow fishermen teased Arbus all day. "How're the womenfolk, Arbus? How's the one with the big red lips?" The lobstermen would dissolve in laughter. I didn't see what was so funny.

I called Jody again. "We need to find Mariah a mate—soon." But when I explained what had happened, Jody said that it was too late. "She's made her choice. It's called imprinting." A swan sometimes thinks a member of another species is its mother or mate. Mariah had imprinted Arbus.

One morning, with daylight barely discernible, we were awakened by a racket at the front door. "Hee, hee, hee," Mariah cried for 15 minutes. "Go ahead and play with her," I growled. As I went back to sleep, Arbus jumped out the door like a first-grader dismissed from class.

Mariah now spent most of her time with us, taking up residence under the big blue spruce. Arbus had thoughtfully provided her with a water bucket and a regular supply of bread crusts.

As autumn advanced, Arbus often came home after nightfall. It is the instinct of a swan to take to water at dark, to avoid predators. But Mariah fought that instinct, pacing in front of our house, hee-hooing worriedly, with a look that said, "He should be home by now." Finally, with darkness, instinct would conquer love, and she'd return to the safety of her pond. When the truck finally came in, we'd hear her trumpet from across the field. Arbus would call back: " 'Night, sweetie. See you in the morning!"

One day as I watched Arbus building traps in his shop with Mariah lying nearby, I understood her gift to him. She provided something he had never known—unconditional love. Arbus had grown up without a father, and his mother had been preoccupied with survival. Even I was there with conditions attached. Not Mariah. No matter how long after dark he came in, and how much anxiety this caused her, she forgave him and greeted him joyously the next morning.

Early November brought the first snowfall. "There shouldn't be a problem," Jody said. "So long as her feet don't freeze and there's shelter she can get into."

When the temperature plunged a few weeks later, Arbus bought lumber to build Mariah a house on the little island in the middle of her pond. Before the house was finished, it snowed again, and Mariah appeared the next morning with her feathers coated with frost. In total seriousness, Arbus asked, "Can we buy her one of those jackets dogs wear?" I looked at his brow, furrowed with worry, and knew that love was insane.

As autumn turned to winter and the islanders moved indoors, I began to feel like Mariah, pacing around waiting for Arbus to come home for supper. But 12 hours of hauling lobster traps is exhausting work, and after eating he'd soon fall asleep. Long, empty evenings would end my long, empty days.

By early December, the gray pounding sea had turned into prison bars for me. "I'm going crazy out here," I said. Knowing there was no life for Arbus in Portland, I suggested a compromise—that we move to Vinalhaven, an island closer to shore with a thousand people, and three ferries a day to the mainland. He could still do his lobstering—and I could get a bit of my own life back again.

But Arbus was unconvinced. "This is where I belong," he said flatly. "I'm not moving." When the seas settled, we loaded my belongings aboard his boat and headed for the mainland.

I have enjoyed the happiness of the world; I have loved.

FRIEDRICH VON SCHILLER

Weeks later, Arbus called to ask if he could visit me in Portland. When he arrived, there was a resentful chill between us, mirroring the blizzard that soon hit Maine. For three days the wind blew out of the northeast at 50 miles an hour, carrying with it more snow than the coast had seen for years.

When the storm was over, Elaine called. "Mariah's missing," she cried. Arbus listened gravely while Elaine recounted how, as the days went by and the truck failed to appear, Mariah had maintained ever-longer vigils in Arbus's front yard. When the storm passed, Elaine had gone out on snowshoes to look for Mariah, but the black swan was nowhere to be found.

Jody had cautioned that Mariah might take refuge in the forest. Arbus left immediately. For three days he searched dense woods and rocky cliffs.

On the morning of his fourth day home, Arbus sat at the kitchen table, staring absently out the window at the big blue spruce. The snowdrift against it had to be at least five feet deep. He felt a chill.

Arbus struggled into his coveralls and boots and waded into the drift. It didn't take him long to find black feathers against the snow.

"I keep telling myself that this is a bird, not a human being," said the voice on the other end of the phone. "It's not as if it were you I found in the snow." Arbus paused. "I wish you were here." I wished I were too.

He buried Mariah at sea, just by the bell buoy that marked the entrance to the harbor where she had come into our lives. Then he came back to Portland. The chill between us was gone, and now I saw how silly we had been to let it ever exist.

At the end of March I told Arbus what I'd heard from Elaine. "The lady on Islesboro moved back to New York and boarded her new swans at an animal kennel," I said. "Why don't we ask to keep them on Matinicus?"

He stared at me. Arbus had heard only one word. "We?"

On the boat ride out to the island the next week I stood next to Arbus. "It's not going to work," he said, and quickly noticed my alarmed expression. "The swans, I mean. Their wings are already cut, so it wouldn't be any good to have them on Vinalhaven. Too many predators."

This time I heard only one word. "Vinalhaven?"

Arbus wrapped his arm over my shoulder. I thought of the swan that had left our lives as suddenly as she'd entered. Twice Mariah had abandoned safety to search for love. Once her quest had brought her new life; the second time had brought her death. But Mariah instinctively knew what Arbus and I, unwilling to abandon the security of our separate lives, had learned only with her death: in the absence of love, safety has no meaning. No matter how tranquil the pond, without love it's a desolate place.

Love rules the court, the camp, the grove,

And men below, and saints above;

For love is heaven, and heaven is love.

SIR WALTER SCOTT

FOR BETTER,
FOR WORSE

BY

ROBERT FULGHUM

A man and woman I know fell in BIG LOVE somewhat later in life than usual. She was thirty-nine. He was forty-seven. Neither had been married before. But they had seen the realities of that sacred state up close among their friends. They were determined to overcome as many potential difficulties as possible by working things out in advance.

A prenuptial agreement over money and property was prepared by lawyers. Preemptive counseling over perceived tensions was provided by a psychologist, who helped them commit all practical promises to paper.

"Get married once, do it right, and live at least agreeably, if not happily, ever after." So they hoped.

Two issues they discussed thoroughly were pets and kids. He agreed, reluctantly, to children if they should come, but said no to pets—and certainly not both.

The man was not enthusiastic about dependent relationships. She, on the other hand, liked taking care of living things. Especially children and dogs.

Okay. They had two daughters in three years. Marriage and family life went along quite well.

The children reached school age. The mother leapt eagerly into the bottomless pool of educational volunteerism. The school needed funds for programs such as art and music. The mother helped organize a major-league auction to raise money. Every family agreed to provide an item for the event.

Remember, the mother was fond of dogs. She had raised dogs all her life. She planned to use her expertise to shop the local puppy pounds to find an unnoticed bargain pooch and shape it up for the auction as her contribution. With a small investment, she would make a tenfold profit for the school. And for a couple of days, at least, there would be a dog in the house.

After a month of looking, she found the wonder dog—the dog of great promise. Male, four months old, black with brown eyes, tall, strong, confident, and very friendly.

To her practiced eye, our mother could see that classy genes had accidentally mixed here. Two purebred dogs of the highest caliber had combined to produce this exceptional animal. Most likely a black Labrador and a Weimaraner, she thought. Perfect.

To those of untutored eye, this mutt looked more like the result of a bad blind date between a Mexican burro and a miniature musk ox.

The fairy dogmother goes to work. The dog is inspected and given shots by a vet. Fitted with an elegant collar and leash. Equipped with a handsome bowl, a ball, and a rawhide bone. Expenses: $50 to the pound, $50 to the vet, $60 for equipment, and $50 for food. A total of $210 on a dog that is going to stay 48 hours before auction time.

The father takes one look and pales. He wouldn't give ten bucks to keep it an hour. "Dog," as the father names it, has a long, thick, rubber club of a tail, legs and feet that remind him of hairy toilet plungers, and is already big enough at four months to bowl over the girls and their mother with its unrestrained enthusiasm.

The father knows this is going to be ONE BIG DOG. Something a zoo might display. Omnivorous, it has left permanent teeth marks on a chair leg, a beeper, and the father's favorite shoes. The father is patient about all of this. After all, it is only a temporary arrangement, and for a good cause.

On a weekend night the school affair gets off to a winning start. Big crowd of parents and many guests who look flush with money. Arty decorations, fine potluck food, a cornucopia of auction items. The mother basks in her triumph.

Dog is placed in the car before going on the auction block so the family can get something to eat. When the father checks on Dog a little later, he finds it methodically chewing the car's seat belts.

After a little wrestling match getting Dog into the mother's arms and up onto the stage, the mother sits in a folding chair, cradling Dog with the solemn tenderness reserved for a child, while the auctioneer describes the animal and all the fine effort and equipment thrown in with the deal.

"What am I bid for this wonderful animal?"

"A hundred dollars over here; $200 on the right; $250 in the middle."

There is a sniffle from the mother. Tears are running down her face. Dog is licking the tears off her cheeks.

In a whisper not really meant for public notice, the mother calls to her husband: "Tom, Tom, I can't sell this dog—I want this dog—he loves me—I love him—oh, Tom."

Every eye in the room is on this soapy drama.

The father feels ill, realizing that the great bowling ball of fate is headed down his alley.

"Please, Tom, please," she whispers.

At that moment, everybody in the room knows who is going to buy the pooch. Dog is going home with Tom.

Having no fear now of being stuck themselves, several men set the bidding on fire. Dog is going to set an auction record. The repeated $100 rise in price is matched by the soft, "Please, Tom," from the stage and Tom's almost inaudible raise in the bidding, five dollars at a time.

There is a long pause somewhere past a thousand dollars—"Going once, going twice . . ."

A sob from the stage.

And so Tom buys himself a dog.

The noble father is applauded as his wife rushes from the stage to throw her arms around his neck. A memorable night for the PTA.

Now I see Tom out being walked by Dog late at night. He's the only one strong enough to control him, and he hates to have the neighbors see him dragged along by the most expensive dog for 100 miles.

Dog has become "McNeill." He is now big enough to plow with. McNeill may be the world's dumbest dog, having been to obedience school twice with no apparent effect.

Tom is still stunned. He can't believe this has happened to him.

He had a deal. Kids or pets, not both.

But the complicating clauses in the fine print of the marriage contract are always unreadable. And always open to revision by forces stronger than a man's ego.

I say he got off light. It could have been ponies or llamas or pot-bellied pigs. The love boat always leaks. And marriage is never a done deal. It would have been something. It always is.

LIGHT AFTER DARK

BY
EDIE CLARK

Not long ago, one August night, I was drawn outside to the brightness of the moon. Though it was almost ten o'clock, I could see the silvery silhouettes of the sheep in my field and the gauzy brilliance of zinnias and marigolds beside the stone wall. There was to be a total eclipse that night, one clearly to be seen. With my flashlight I went down the root-stepped path to the narrow wooden dock where I keep the rowboat.

It is something Paul and I would have done. Often we went out before sunup, rowing through mist that rose from the water like angel's hair. We listened for loons and came across great blue herons breakfasting in the shallows. We rowed until the sun popped up from behind the hills that rim this long thin lake.

I am just getting used to the boat's lightness with only one of us aboard. Finishing it was part of Paul's work during chemotherapy. He would come home from the hospital and plane and sand the hull, then coat it, layer on layer, with high-sheen varnish. The drugs made him sick, but he hid his discomfort and carried on as if nothing were happening.

By the time I reached the middle of the lake, a good chunk of darkness had pushed its way into the moon. Yellow light poured through the windows of the shoreline cottages, wavering on the waters like banners. I shipped the oars and sat still.

All around I could hear screen doors slam and voices drift toward me. Others, too, wanted to see the eclipse. Behind me I heard laughter, and though I saw no lights, I knew a boat must be there. Darkness moved farther into the moon.

My little boat drifted in a wide, slow circle. There had been a breeze when I started out, but it had died, and now the water stretched out flat beyond me, black as ink. I leaned back against the seat. High in the center of the sky, the moon had gone blood-red. A hair-thin crescent of light remained. I watched it close shut—the moon was fully dark.

On shore a firecracker popped. A hoot, and then the voices faded, doors slammed, and one by one the cottages vanished into blackness. I snapped on the flashlight to read my watch: midnight.

I lay back, face to the heavens. Paul had died almost three months before. He was only thirty-nine. Since his death there had been times when I felt this same kind of darkness, even on bright, sunlit days. Though I drifted alone in the boat, I felt the weight of him near me. I felt the pressure of his hand in mine.

Suddenly, a fish plopped. The air moved again and brought current back to the water, making tiny waves tap the boat gently. A thumbnail of light opened from the other side of the moon. It grew wider, and light fell back down onto the water with the glitter of stars dropped to earth.

I knew then why I had come. Not to see the earth go dark, but to see the light come back again. I sat up and set the oars into the water. With strong, sweeping strokes, I rowed back to the dock in the broadening light.

It grew wider, and light fell back down onto the water

A DIFFERENT KIND OF
LOVE STORY

BY

SAM MOSES

On most Wednesday evenings after supper, Lester and Ivadene Claycomb climb into their 34,000-pound, $52,000 Kenworth diesel rig and begin the long haul from their home in Duncansville, Pennsylvania, to Homestead, Florida. Stopping only for meals, coffee, and a few hours' sleep in the bunk of the cab, they arrive Friday morning. After the trailer is unloaded, they drive across town to pick up a load of produce—watermelons, crates of lettuce, sacks of potatoes—and head home again, arriving Saturday night after a round-trip of over 2500 miles.

Monday morning, often as early as six o'clock, Lester walks across the grass to the large garage behind their house where, alone, he continues the eternal chore of maintaining the couple's four diesel rigs. Ivadene, meanwhile, attacks the laundry and housework, and in the afternoon takes on the company's business: scheduling trips, dickering with freight dispatchers, paying bills, keeping the books. On many Tuesday afternoons they make a 300-mile round-trip in the Kenworth to York, Pennsylvania, to deliver local produce, returning home just before dawn. And on Wednesday nights they usually leave for Florida again.

Lester Claycomb is seventy-three years old; Ivadene is sixty-seven. They have been married 51 years and have worked together in the interstate trucking business for 47 of those years. Their story is not one of two downtrodden oldsters forced by the system to work their fingers to the bone, but of two vital, energetic, useful people who love their work—and each other.

They appear to be opposites. Ivadene is taller than Lester and ten pounds heavier. She's a talker who loves an audience; Lester is so laconic that he sometimes seems mute. But these differences are superficial; in their hearts, where it counts, they are very much alike.

It is a Wednesday evening in January, and Lester and Ivadene are en route to Florida. There is a feeling of relief in the truck, a tacit sigh in the air. There is always that feeling at the beginning of a trip; they work so hard at home that their first hours in the truck are actually relaxing. The cab is their cocoon.

A light snow falls softly as they head for Interstate 70. The windshield wipers flap like a metronome; amber lights glow on the instrument panel, warming the atmosphere in the cab. There's a CB radio, but it is difficult to imagine Lester talking into it. "Aw, it just makes noise," he says. And that is about all Lester will say for the next few hours.

The road is a place where Ivadene is silent as well. "If Lester talks to me, I answer him," she says. "But I don't bother him. We can ride for a hundred miles without saying a word. I'm watching the road all the time, though. When the old man starts getting heavy-eyed, weaving around the road about two in the morning, I say, 'Okay, it's time to pull over.' "

The bunk above and behind the seats in the cab is dark and cozy, and big enough for two if they cuddle. "We crawl around there like two-year-olds," says Ivadene. In the bunk are two goosedown sleeping bags and two foam pillows. It is likely the most intimate, secure, and

even romantic spot they have, and their moments there are something special, something most married couples would envy.

Lester and Ivadene began dating when he was twenty-one and she was fifteen. Says Ivadene, "Lester was the jokester type; even when he was telling the truth he had a grin on him. My daddy didn't know how to take him."

A year later, in February 1928, they were married, and four years later their first child—Althea—was born. That same year Lester and Ivadene went into the trucking business.

They started with one truck, the bed of which they built themselves: Lester hammered and Ivadene held. The truck was longer than their garage, so they ignored the snow that blew in the open door while they worked, wearing extra coveralls. After a driver Lester had hired for a short haul wrecked the truck, they rebuilt it and traded it for a semi.

Over the next 20 years, six more children were born to Ivadene and Lester. On many trips Ivadene took at least one of her children along; other times she stayed home and Lester took one of the children himself. The fondest childhood memories of daughter Judy, now thirty-one, are the days she spent traveling with her daddy, standing up in the seat next to him as he drove along, high above the other cars on the highway, her arm around his shoulder.

At its peak, in 1948, the Claycombs' business included 14 trucks and 19 trailers, and they employed 14 drivers. "We've been through a lot," says Ivadene. "We've seen some rough times, had a lot of hard luck and heartaches. After forty-seven years I sometimes get tired and wish we didn't have to live such a slavish life. But we've never known anything but trucks. We wouldn't know what to do with ourselves if we quit.

"I'm still always available if the old man needs help in the garage," she continues. "I'm right down there with him under the truck. Last trip from Florida we unloaded a full load of produce in two hours flat. Lester told me to take it a little easy, and I said, 'You're a good one to talk, because you ain't stoppin' either!' He hasn't taken a day off in forty-seven years."

A lifetime of hard work can be read in Lester's hands. Emerging from forearms as muscular as a weight lifter's, the hands are impressively strong from thousands of hours of twisting wrenches, shifting the 13 gears on his trucks, and wrestling with steering wheels the size of manhole covers. The fingers are so thick there seems to be almost no space between them, with knuckles hard like stones. They look too clubby to manage a shirt button, but these are the same fingers that have gently changed the diapers of an infant daughter in the bunk of a rig at some rest spot along the highway.

"I can't do without Pap," says Ivadene. "I can take care of business, but I have to have a good mechanic." The statement clearly applies to their life as well as their work. Lester understands trucks, Ivadene understands people. He trusts her and isn't threatened by a woman doing what she can do better than he. She, in return, is unfailingly supportive. It is truly a liberated relationship, something more sophisticated people often search for all their lives.

"We've had ups and downs in our marriage," says Ivadene. "But we've toughed it out for fifty-one years. *Cooperation*: that's what it takes. You got to give and take. Be honest and learn to agree. Marriage can be a wonderful thing if two people understand each other."

"They don't realize how happy they are working together," says daughter Judy. "They don't have a lot of money, but if they did, they wouldn't even know it. My mother really loves that man; my father could go out and dig ditches, and she would be right with him. I would like to end my own life with that kind of bond."

"It's nice to have a partner, is what it is," says Ivadene.

THE MARRIAGE MYSTERY

BY

KEN GROSS

"So," I said, "how do you like them?"

"How do I like what?" replied the wife.

"The new glasses."

She looked up, surprised. She said something odd: "I didn't know you wear glasses."

"Maybe," I quipped, "you need glasses."

She paused, possibly a second, and said, "I do wear glasses."

The woman I had fallen for—a case of love at first spectacle-less sight—did not wear glasses then. In that first indelible moment, she had brown hair, an 18-inch waist, and unblemished skin. And in that same glazed, first blush, she looked at me with something approaching uncritical rapture. All these things were petrified forever in perpetual first-memories.

I was aware that she now has tinsels of gray in her hair—and that she keeps her waist discreetly hidden under untucked shirts.

But lovers have a pact. We agree to see each other through a benign lens of revisionist affection.

194

"As far as I am concerned," she said, "you do not wear glasses. I don't think of you with glasses."

True. I do not think of her with glasses, either. I do not see the effects of time. Not the physical changes. She is still the twenty-four-year-old sprite who stood before the pigeonhole mailboxes of our office and, after a long pause, turned and asked with absolute sincerity, "What's my name again?"

Such are the clear impressions that last.

"What do you make of it?" I asked.

"Make of what?"

"The fact that we don't think of each other with glasses." She didn't miss a comic beat.

"We don't see each other anymore," she said.

At least it's what I credit her with saying. Sometimes I think she said what I say she said. Sometimes I put words in her mouth. If she didn't say it, she could have.

It happens to people who are blinded and deafened by high emotional stakes. We attribute things to each other. We work like mad to defend each other's image. I send a gift in her name. I make excuses. No one speaks ill of her in my presence.

You can see a certain potential for confusion and trouble here. But there's no way out. People who live together—live together deeply—surrender pieces of themselves. They blend in ways one would not think possible. (She might see the possibilities, but I don't.) I don't really know if it was my wife or I who first discovered Charles Kuralt. Or Joseph Heller.

It doesn't matter.

See, part of the whole thing is to show her, to discover it again. When we went to Paris for her first time, it was as if I'd never been there before. I tasted it all fresh again with her. Movies I have seen 20 times, which I couldn't bear to watch alone, I watch with her. She thought *The*

Longest Day was another war movie until she saw it and, maybe, sensed something else from watching it with me.

I know that if she likes something, I will give it an extra try because I trust her judgment. After I finished reading *Something Happened,* I read it again when she did.

Early in our marriage she resented this. She would hide books and accuse me of violating her intellectual privacy. But gradually she accepted my presence in the secret rooms of her mind.

Some people, poor devils, see it as settled boredom—the thing that happens when husbands finish the sentences begun by wives. It is the looks across tables that do not have to be spelled out. It is the opinion about Sylvester Stallone and Wayne Newton that goes without saying.

It is, in short, a marriage in the most profound sense. The kind in which both parties regard each other through rose-colored glasses.

I met in the street a very poor young man

who was in love. His hat was old, his coat

was threadbare, the water passed through

his shoes and the stars through his soul.

VICTOR HUGO

MY GIRL, MY WIFE

BY

CHARLTON HESTON

I entered Northwestern University in the fall of 1941—a shy, skinny, ill-dressed boy on a $300 scholarship from the Winnetka Community Theater. For the first two or three days in my theater course, I sat behind a girl named Lydia Clarke. All I saw was her tumbling mane of black Irish hair, which made me tremble. She bent over her desk, taking notes. I sat bemused, taking note only of her.

Between classes I made terse, offhand remarks—"Hi there. How ya doin'?" But I couldn't figure out how to advance the relationship. I'd never even been on a date. Girls expected to be taken out and bought hamburgers and Cokes and taken home in cars. I didn't have any money. I didn't drive a car or know how to dance. Girls? I didn't have a clue.

Fate, as they say, took a hand: Lydia and I were cast in the same bill of plays. I was in *Francesca da Rimini*, playing a medieval lover, all tights and curled hair and daggers at the belt. Lydia was in a moody English piece called *The Madras House*. During dress rehearsal—could she have been nudging fate along?—Lydia asked me how to speak her opening line. She told me she was to enter and say, "Minnie, my frog is dead!"

Well, of course I knew how that line should be read. I had firm ideas about all the performances. This was conversation I knew. I just had no idea how to stop.

On opening night my medieval bit was first, and I decided I was terrible. As I brooded in a corner of the dressing room, Lydia came in and said, "I thought you were marvelous!"

Cary Grant would have thought of 20 funny or engaging replies. I stuck out my tongue.

In an infinity of female wisdom, Lydia neither walked out nor hit me. Finally I said in a strangled voice, "What I mean is, ah, I would like to talk to you about it. Could we go and, ah, have some coffee?"

Yes, she would like that (this to the music of the spheres). But later, as we walked to the coffee shop, I realized I had no money. Not a nickel. I couldn't tell the celestial beauty beside me. All I could do was silently pray that I'd find a pal I could hit up for a loan. I did: Bill Sweeney, who lent me a quarter. May his name be written in the Golden Book.

Lydia and I had tea, because it would last longer (you got more hot water free). We sat there for some two hours, talking about everything. After I left her at the dorm, I ran home along the dark streets, saying, "I love her, I love her," over and over. I did, too.

Never doubt that this can happen. I'd barely spoken to her before that night, but I knew absolutely. What are the odds: one in a hundred, a thousand? It happened to me.

The fall passed in a hazy mix of work and love. Then, on December 7, 1941, the Japanese attacked Pearl Harbor. Every healthy male between eighteen and forty-five knew where he'd be before long: in uniform.

I enlisted in the Army Air Forces. During the six months before I was called up, Lydia and I continued to share classes, act, and work in stage crews together. "In love" is an inadequate description, at least for me. Try "obsessed." But that was from my end. I don't think Lydia was even in love at that point. She kept me at arm's length, waiting to see if I might ripen into an actual human being.

But she did go out with me, so she must have been drawn to me a little. Since I had no money, we seldom went out on real dates. We walked along the lakefront a lot. I remember once it snowed, and she took my arm. I never moved my elbow the whole 40 minutes we walked, with the flakes whirling down, coating her glove and the sleeve of my jacket. In the spring we often stood beside a lilac bush at school, embracing for ten minutes at a time.

By my last weeks on campus, I was preoccupied with getting Lydia into bed or married to me. She rejected both options with adamantine resolve. She had no intention of getting pregnant or wed: she was determined to get her degree.

Desperately, I fell back on the ploy soldiers have used for centuries. "You realize you may never see me again. We must have something to carry in our hearts! It may be years, it may be never!" It was a heartbreaking performance, not least because I meant it, but it never dented her resolve.

One afternoon we were down in the school basement, silk-screening a set of theater posters. "I got a letter from this boy I knew in high school," Lydia said. "He's coming to town for a few days. Pete."

"Pete?"

"I thought I might see him. He's going in the Navy."

"The Navy?"

"We might have dinner . . . with other people, of course. At that place on Ridge Road. Not a date."

"No! I mean, of course, note a date. Sure, I guess . . . sure."

I had blown it, but all was not lost. She might not be willing to marry me, yet, but I was not going to lose this girl five days before I checked in for World War II! The night of Pete's visit, I bullied a friend into letting me borrow his car. "For one hour, for God's sake. Of course I have a license!" (I didn't.)

All the way to the restaurant where the nefarious Pete was plotting to steal my girl, I rehearsed a speech designed to win her heart. I avoided disaster driving the car and strode confidently into the restaurant, where I saw Lydia seated at a large table. Everyone turned to look at me . . . and I forgot my speech. Every word.

The silence lengthened. Stepping to the table, I took Lydia's hand and said, "Come with me." And she did.

I believe with all my heart that the rest of my life began with that moment. That boyish, quixotic disruption of a dinner is the most important single action I've ever taken. I remain proud of it and eternally grateful to my girl—as she surely became, irreversibly, when she stood and walked out of the restaurant, holding my hand.

After I left for basic training, I redoubled my efforts to get Lydia to marry me. "Just think, darling," I wrote, "if we're married and I get killed, you get $10,000 free and clear." This appeal, eminently rational to my Scots soul, failed to move her.

Exhausted by the grind of basic training, I gave up even mentioning marriage in my letters. One day I shambled back to my barracks after hours on the obstacle course to find a yellow envelope on my bunk. "HAVE DECIDED TO ACCEPT YOUR PROPOSAL," the telegram said. "LOVE, LYDIA."

So she came down to the piney woods of Greensboro, North Carolina, to marry me. A two-day pass was the most I could wangle. I raced into town, where I got us a room and spent my private's pay on a $12 ring.

I was a gangly kid in uniform. But Lydia, in a marvelous violet bridal suit, was a vision that still shimmers in my mind. As we walked to the church, a shower opened over us. Who cared? We ran laughing up the steps and inside to the altar.

Lydia and I have now celebrated our golden wedding anniversary. That's a long time. But half a century, two children, and one wondrous grandson later, it seems no more than a time-tick since I stood beside my girl—my wife—in that Carolina church.

Those who love deeply never grow old; they

may die of old age, but they die young.

ARTHUR WING PINERO

The old
know
what
loving
truly
means;
the
young
can only

guess.

A KISS FOR KATE

BY
PHYLLIS VOLKENS

*E*very afternoon when I came on duty as the evening nurse, I would walk the halls of the nursing home, pausing at each door to chat and observe. Often, Kate and Chris, their big scrapbooks in their laps, would be reminiscing over the photos. Proudly, Kate showed me pictures of bygone years: Chris tall, blond, handsome. Kate pretty, dark-haired, laughing. Two young lovers smiling through the passing seasons. How lovely they looked now, sitting there, the light shining on their white heads, their time-wrinkled faces smiling at remembrances of the years, caught and held forever in the scrapbooks.

How little the young know of loving, I'd think. How foolish to think they have a monopoly on such a precious commodity. The old know what loving truly means; the young can only guess.

Kate and Chris were always together—in the dining room, the lounge, strolling around the big porches and lawns, always holding hands. As we staff members ate our evening meal, sometimes Kate and Chris would walk slowly by the dining-room doors. Then conversation would turn to a discussion of the couple's love and devotion, and what would happen when one of them died. We knew Chris was the strong one, and Kate was dependent upon him.

How would Kate function if Chris were to die first? we often wondered.

Bedtime followed a ritual. When I brought the evening medication, Kate would be sitting in her chair, in nightgown and slippers, awaiting my arrival. Under the watchful eyes of Chris and myself, Kate would take her pill, then carefully Chris would help her from chair to bed and tuck the covers in around her frail body.

Observing this act of love, I would think for the thousandth time, *Good heavens, why don't nursing homes have double beds for married couples?* All their lives they have slept together, but in a nursing home, they're expected to sleep in single beds. Overnight they're deprived of a comfort of a lifetime.

How very foolish such policies are, I would think as I watched Chris reach up and turn off the light above Kate's bed. Then tenderly he would bend, and they would kiss gently. Chris would pat her cheek, and both would smile. He would pull up the side rail on her bed, and only then would he turn and accept his own medication. As I walked into the hall, I could hear Chris say, "Good night, Kate," and her returning voice, "Good night, Chris," while the space of an entire room separated their two beds.

I had been off duty two days and when I returned, the first news I heard was, "Chris died yesterday morning."

"How?"

"A heart attack. It happened quickly."

"How's Kate?"

"Bad."

I went into Kate's room. She sat in her chair, motionless, hands in her lap, staring. Taking her hands in mine, I said, "Kate, it's Phyllis."

Her eyes never shifted; she only stared. I placed my hand under her chin and slowly turned her head so she had to look at me.

"Kate, I just found out about Chris. I'm so sorry."

At the word "Chris," her eyes came back to life. She looked at me, puzzled, as though wondering how I had suddenly appeared. "Kate, it's me, Phyllis. I'm so sorry about Chris."

Recognition and remembrance flooded her face. Tears welled up and slid down her cheeks. "Chris is gone," she whispered.

"I know," I said. "I know."

We pampered Kate for a while, letting her eat in her room, surrounding her with special attention. Then gradually the staff worked her back into the old schedule. Often, as I went past her room, I would observe Kate sitting in her chair, scrapbooks on her lap, gazing sadly at pictures of Chris.

Bedtime was the worst part of the day for Kate. Although she had been granted her request to move from her bed to Chris's bed, and although the staff chatted and laughed with her as they tucked her in for the night, still Kate remained silent and sadly withdrawn. Passing her room an hour after she had been tucked in, I'd find her wide awake, staring at the ceiling.

The weeks passed, and bedtime wasn't any better. She seemed so restless, so insecure. *Why?* I wondered. *Why this time of day more than the other hours?*

Then one night as I walked into her room, only to find the same wide-awake Kate, I said impulsively, "Kate, could it be you miss your good-night kiss?" Bending down, I kissed her wrinkled cheek.

It was as though I had opened the floodgates. Tears coursed down her face; her hands gripped mine. "Chris always kissed me good night," she cried.

"I know," I whispered.

"I miss him so, all those years he kissed me good night." She paused while I wiped the tears. "I just can't seem to go to sleep without his kiss."

She looked up at me, eyes brimming. "Oh, thank you for giving me a kiss."

A small smile turned up the corners of her mouth. "You know," she said confidentially, "Chris used to sing me a song."

"He did?"

"Yes"—her white head nodded—"and I lie here at night and think about it."

"How did it go?"

Kate smiled, held my hand, and cleared her throat. Then her voice, small with age but still melodious, lifted softly in song:

> *So kiss me, my sweet, and so let us part.*
> *And when I grow too old to dream,*
> *That kiss will live in my heart.*

Young love is a flame—very pretty—often very hot and fierce, but still only light and flickering. The love of the older and disciplined heart is as coals, deep-burning, unquenchable.

HENRY WARD BEECHER

HOUSE ON THE LAKE

BY

MIKE ROYKO

When the two of them started spending weekends at the quiet Wisconsin lake, they were young and had little money. Her relatives let them use a tiny cottage in a wooded hollow a mile or so from the water.

He worked odd hours, so often they wouldn't get there until after midnight on a Friday. But if the mosquitoes weren't out, they'd go for a moonlight swim, then rest with their backs against a tree and drink wine and talk about their future.

One summer the young man bought an old motorboat. They'd ride along the shoreline, looking at the houses and wondering what it would be like to have a place on the water. He'd just shake his head; these houses cost more than he could ever afford.

Years passed. They had kids. After a while they didn't go to the little cottage as often. Finally her relatives sold the place.

Then he got lucky in his work, making more money than he ever dreamed they'd have. Remembering those weekends, they went back and bought a cedar house on the water. The place was surrounded by big old trees, and the land sloped gently down to the shore. It was perfect.

They hadn't known summers could be that good. In the mornings he'd go fishing before it was light. She'd sleep until the birds woke her. Then he'd make breakfast, and they'd eat omelets on the deck.

They got to know the chipmunks, the squirrels, and a woodpecker who took over their biggest tree. They got to know the grocer, the butcher who smoked his own bacon, the farmer who sold them vine-ripened tomatoes.

The best part of their day was dusk. She loved sunsets. They'd always stop to watch the sun go down, changing the color of the lake from blue to purple, to silver and black. One evening he made up a small poem:

> *The sun rolls down*
> *like a golden tear*
> *Another day,*
> *Another day*
> *gone.*

She told him it was sad, but that she liked it.

What she didn't like was October, even with the beautiful colors and evenings in front of the fireplace. She was a summer person. The cold wind wasn't her friend.

In November they would store the boat, take down the hammock, lock everything tight, and drive back to the city. She'd always sigh as they left.

Finally spring would come, and when they knew the ice on the lake was gone, they'd be back. She'd throw open the doors and windows and let in the fresh air. Then she'd go out and greet the chipmunks and the woodpeckers.

Every summer seemed better than the last. The sunsets seemed more spectacular. And more precious.

Then one weekend he went alone to close the place down for the winter.

He worked quickly, trying not to let himself think that this particular chair had been her favorite, that the hammock had been her Christmas gift to him, that the house on the lake had been his gift to her.

He didn't work quickly enough. He was still there at sunset. It was a great burst of orange, the kind she had loved best.

He tried, but he couldn't watch it alone. Not through tears. So he turned his back on it, went inside, drew the draperies, locked the door, and drove away.

Later there would be a "for sale" sign out front. Maybe a couple who loved to quietly watch sunsets together would like it. He hoped so.

Mike Royko wrote this memorial to his first wife, Carol, after she died in 1979. The longtime Chicago newspaper columnist died in 1997.

Love is friendship that has caught fire.

ANN LANDERS

THE SPY AND THE PROFESSOR

BY
MICHAEL BOWKER

As the jet dropped gently through the blue China skies, Larry Engelmann could see the ancient city of Nanjing shimmering below in the late-summer heat. "This will be the greatest adventure of my life," Engelmann, a history professor at California's San Jose State, had written to a friend. He had no idea how prophetic his words were.

Engelmann had been teaching for two decades and often felt that he had fallen into a "tweedy, academic rut." In late 1987, when Johns Hopkins University offered him a teaching position on an exchange program at Nanjing University, he jumped at the chance.

He could never have suspected that while at Nanjing University he would come under intense scrutiny by the People's Liberation Army (PLA). Because of work he was doing for a book on Vietnam, the PLA became convinced that Engelmann was working for the CIA.

Oblivious to the fact that he was being watched, Engelmann spent several days walking around Nanjing, taking hundreds of photographs. Gregarious by nature, the six-foot, two-inch, 200-pound, curly-haired professor tried to talk to anybody who spoke English. It was unlikely behavior for a spy, but the PLA decided he was a master of deception. Engelmann had also worked as a journalist, confirming their suspicions. (In China, all journalists are expected to gather information for their government.)

One day after class, Engelmann invited one of his students, a bright, attractive woman named Xu Meihong (pronounced Shu May Hong), to walk with him to the post office.

Meihong, he discovered, was highly intelligent, spoke good English, and was more than a little inquisitive. She asked him questions on an array of subjects, including military strategy.

In early November, Engelmann and another instructor toured Beijing for a few days with Meihong as their guide. One night in a restaurant, Engelmann saw Meihong in candlelight and "for the first time," he told friends later, "I saw how beautiful she was." He was, he realized, starting to care for her deeply. And Meihong seemed to encourage his attention, even though liaisons between Chinese and Americans were forbidden.

Born in 1963, Xu Meihong had grown up in a rural area about 50 miles from Nanjing. An excellent student, she—like many Chinese young people—dreamed of joining the PLA, whose members enjoyed power, privilege, and status. She studied international relations and English, and when the PLA began to recruit women for more sensitive jobs, she was one of the first chosen.

She moved to Nanjing and underwent extensive PLA training. She studied Russian and English, military history and aircraft design. She also learned to shoot various weapons. Self-assured and assertive, she rapidly worked her way up.

In the autumn of 1988, Meihong received her first assignment—to spy on Engelmann while a student in his history class.

As the weeks went by that fall, Meihong began to see Engelmann as a warm, gentle man, perhaps even a bit naïve. She watched him helping the poor Chinese students get American textbooks for free and appreciated his generosity. She had been told all her life that all American men were playboys and not to be trusted. Now she saw it was a lie.

Meihong told her superiors she didn't think he was a spy at all. The PLA bugged her room.

A few days later Meihong, distraught, went to Engelmann's apartment. "Larry, I am not a student," she said. "I am a PLA officer, assigned to spy on you. They think you are CIA, but I know you are not. I have to tell you this so it does not destroy our relationship."

Engelmann laughed uproariously. She had played practical jokes on him before.

The next day she returned to his room and disappeared into the bathroom. She reappeared in a green and red military uniform, certain it would convince him.

"This is my PLA uniform," she said. "I am an army lieutenant," and added that his phone was tapped and his mail routinely opened.

To Engelmann, the notion seemed absurd. He thought her uniform was a Halloween costume. Then he did what had become second nature to him in China. He took her picture, a mistake he would soon regret.

Later Engelmann added the film to a couple of other rolls he wanted to develop and took them to a photo shop. Neither he nor any of the U.S. instructors knew that agents examine every photograph taken by foreigners in the city. What PLA officers saw on Engelmann's film shocked them—one of their own officers, blowing her cover to an American professor they believed was a CIA spy.

Just before midnight on December 2, Meihong was still awake, trying to think of a way to persuade Engelmann of her true identity, when a PLA colleague called, said she badly needed to talk, and would send a jeep over. Meihong got into the jeep and talked amicably with the two men she assumed were taking her to her friend's apartment.

Suddenly the jeep veered off course and stopped in front of a military prison. Meihong was led to a bare room where several men in PLA uniforms waited. They showed her the picture Engelmann had taken and accused her of treason. She was interrogated for several hours, then taken to a small, filthy room.

During the days that followed, she was beaten and interrogated with regularity. She was not allowed blankets or warm clothing. She was told to sleep, then awakened whenever she dozed. Soon her PLA interrogators demanded that she sign a nine-page "confession" that Engelmann had repeatedly raped her—a crime punishable by death in China.

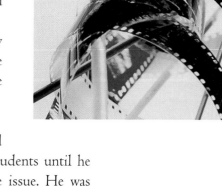

Meihong knew that if she signed the confession, she might never leave the prison. She was determined to hold out for her own sake and for Engelmann's.

For two agonizing months, Meihong lived in the tiny room, not knowing if each day would be her last. She could hear the rifles of a firing squad, and sometimes she was forced to watch executions.

When Meihong did not appear in class or respond to his phone calls, Engelmann questioned the other students until he was finally warned by Chinese authorities to drop the issue. He was joined in his concerns by American students, who glued Meihong's picture on milk bottles emblazoned with the words "Have you seen this woman?"

In January 1989, Engelmann was told that Meihong had signed a confession charging him with rape.

He was now threatened with imprisonment, and friends warned him to leave China. On Sunday, February 19, Engelmann flew to Hong Kong, but not before asking everyone he knew at the school to continue looking for Meihong.

The pressure on Meihong steadily increased. After she was interrogated for hours, former friends from her training days would enter the room and try to get her to confide in them. For her birthday they had baked her a cake and held a small party. During the celebration they told her she could go home if she confessed. She refused, and the party abruptly ended.

In the middle of February, the third month of her captivity, Meihong was exiled without explanation to a small, isolated farming area to be "reeducated through labor." Knowing it might be years before she would be allowed to leave, she had but one choice—escape. Her only hope was to return to Nanjing and find Engelmann.

When the local police were celebrating the Chinese New Year, she slipped away on a boat and floated for two days down the Yangtze River. She longed to go directly to Nanjing to find Engelmann, but knew she had to remain for a time in rural areas where she wouldn't be recognized.

For weeks Meihong moved from one small town to the next. Finally, broke and desperate, she smuggled herself aboard a crowded train for an 18-hour trip to Beijing.

She had been warned never to contact Engelmann, but she called his number immediately. A woman answered and said she had never heard of him. Meihong learned from friends that Engelmann had left the country months before. She was crushed by the thought that he had deserted her.

Between a man and his wife nothing ought to rule but love.

WILLIAM PENN

In mid-August, Meihong met a Chinese student who was about to attend a student exchange program at the University of Kansas. She gave the student her phone number and Engelmann's at San Jose State.

One afternoon in late August, a secretary stopped Engelmann as he was leaving San Jose State after classes.

"You had a strange call this morning from a Chinese man in Lawrence, Kansas, something about 'Mayron,' or something," she said. "He left his number."

Engelmann raced upstairs to his office. He excitedly dialed the number. Nobody answered. Engelmann dialed the number every ten minutes for the next four hours until the Chinese student finally answered and gave him Meihong's number.

It was early in the morning in China when Engelmann was patched through to Beijing.

"Xu Meihong?" he almost shouted.

"Wei, yes," she said.

"I love you!"

She burst into tears.

They wrote and called each other frequently over the next few weeks. Engelmann got her admitted to San Jose State, but months went by and Chinese authorities refused to grant her a student visa.

Frustrated, Engelmann bought a plane ticket to Shanghai, planning to reenter China secretly and marry Meihong and force Chinese officials to let her leave. His friends pleaded with him not to go. Meihong could still be a PLA agent enticing him back into a trap, they said. To go back to China would be a leap of faith that could land him in prison for the rest of his life.

Engelmann arrived in Shanghai on January 7, 1990. While making his way through the crowd, he saw Meihong, and his heart stopped.

Next to her was a man in a military uniform. After all this, he wondered, had she betrayed him?

"Who is the man?" Engelmann asked.

"A friend," she said. "He is our driver. Please, trust me."

They had to move quickly. Their plan was to marry and for Engelmann to escape the country that same day with the marriage certificate. If they were caught, they feared authorities would destroy the certificate and imprison them both.

Because they still needed certain documents, Meihong had to return to the town where she was born, which was several hours by train from Shanghai. They spent a week collecting the necessary documents. Eight hours after they were married, Engelmann was in the air with the marriage certificate in his pocket. Both believed that the Chinese would soon be forced to allow Meihong to emigrate now that she was married to an American citizen.

They were wrong. Weeks went by, and Meihong heard nothing about her request to leave.

In San Jose, an outraged Engelmann flooded Congress, the State Department, the White House, and the Chinese embassy with letters. California Representative Tom Campbell (R., Palo Alto) and California Senator Pete Wilson promised to help. Engelmann wrote to Barbara Bush, Pat Nixon, Henry Kissinger, and everyone else he could think of who had ever been associated with China.

Months went by and the Chinese gave no sign of letting Meihong go. Desperate, Engelmann began making plans to return to China and smuggle her out. He was putting together the final details in early December when he received a phone call from the State Department.

"Something is happening with Meihong," the caller said excitedly. "Just sit tight."

On a cold, sunny morning a few days later, Engelmann's phone rang. It was Meihong. Her passport had been approved.

Today, from the window of their modern high-rise apartment, Meihong can see the San Jose State campus. She got her first job in the spring of 1991, teaching Southeast Asian refugees the basics of American life, such as banking, shopping, and looking for work.

Why Chinese authorities released Meihong may never be clear. Engelmann thinks it might be because they did not want the case to become an issue in Washington after the Tiananmen Square massacre. What matters now is their future.

"It hasn't been easy, especially at first," Meihong says. "But Larry helped me realize that America is a country of all nationalities, that it belongs to people who love freedom, not to a race of people called Americans."

LOVE IN AN UNLIKELY SEASON

BY

MARJORIE HOLMES

On a bright February morning my telephone rang. "Marjorie Holmes?" a rich male voice announced. "You saved my life. I love you!"

Some nut, I thought—but I didn't hang up. As a writer you learn to listen. His name, he said, was George Schmieler, and he was a doctor from Pittsburgh. He'd lost his wife eight months before. On New Year's Eve, wild with grief and on the verge of suicide, he'd found my book *I've Got to Talk to Somebody, God.*

"It was among her things," he said. "I read it that night, and it made me realize how precious life is."

He was calling from his son's home in Silver Spring, Maryland. "I knew you lived in the Washington area. I found out your married name, and began to dial." Finally, he had reached a man who said, "Why, yes, her husband was my cousin, who died a year ago. Her number's right here."

"If you are still free," George said, "may I see you?"

I was pleased and touched. But unfortunately, I told him, I was about to leave on a two-week speaking trip.

222

"I'll wait!" he said. "Just promise you'll call as soon as you get back." His voice was cheery but urgent. "We haven't got that much time."

When I returned, my mailbox was stuffed with envelopes postmarked Silver Spring. They contained romantic notes, jokes, poems, and items marked simply "interesting."

I called him, as promised, and suggested meeting somewhere for dinner. But he insisted on coming to get me.

It was my first date in a very long time. I felt expectant, curious.

I thought about what I'd been doing on New Year's Eve, when George had found my book. Watching couples on television dancing, I was lonely. "You need to get out," my daughter Melanie chided me. Her tone was teasing, but her eyes were sweet with caring. "Much as we all loved Daddy, we know things were very hard for you. He was sick so long, and . . ." She hesitated. "You deserve to be happy!"

George arrived an hour early that evening. While Melanie and her husband, Haris, entertained him, I rushed to do my makeup, trying not to panic. Finally, I took a deep breath and joined them.

A tall, handsome man leaped to his feet, clutching an armful of roses. He had curly gray hair, a mustache, and the bluest eyes I'd ever seen. Beaming like a schoolboy, he handed me the flowers.

"You're so little!" George exclaimed, but he sounded delighted. "I could put you in my pocket."

"And you're so tall!"

"Never mind, we'll match."

He held out his arms, and suddenly we were hugging.

We ate at a restaurant near my home. He was gallant, poised, and charming—and also very funny. Never had I felt more comfortable with anyone. As we walked to the car after dinner, he began to sing songs that we both remembered, in the sweetest male voice I had ever heard.

Later, while I made coffee, he opened his worn doctor's bag to show me his family pictures. His wife, Carolyn—slim, fair, and serene. Two attractive sons and a lovely daughter. George and Carolyn on Florida beaches where they vacationed every winter, and on cruises to Bermuda. "We always put our marriage first," George explained. "But we also spent plenty of time with the children at our Lake Erie cottage every summer."

"My goodness, when did you practice medicine?" I asked.

"Between vacations," he said with a laugh. "And I worked hard. Work and play, love and pray. These are words I've always tried to live by. Love is the most important—to love your wife and children next to God.

"If I didn't love God first," he said, "I couldn't love other people so much." George paused, his voice unsteady. "The way I loved Carolyn. Or the way I love you now." To my surprise, he kissed me.

I was thrilled but bewildered. Unsure of myself, I couldn't think what to say except, "That's beautiful. And your wife must have shared the same philosophy."

"Oh, she was wonderful." He went on to describe their marriage.

Carolyn had been not only his sweetheart and companion, he told me, but also his secretary and nurse. When she died suddenly at their summer cottage, he went into shock for months.

Then he found my book. "It told me you, too, had suffered," he said, "that a lot of people suffer, but with God's help we can and must go on."

Gone was his former aplomb. "Would you consider marrying me?" he asked, with pleading eyes.

I shook my head. "No, George. You're still in love with your wife. And I could never be the kind of wife she was to you."

"But the past is gone," he said with emotion. "Something happened the minute I heard your voice. It was like waking from a long nightmare. And when I actually saw you tonight! It's not your book, it's you, the wonderful time we've had just in these past few hours. We need each other. Please, at least make an effort to know me."

I explained how difficult that would be. He was practicing in Pittsburgh. I was busy with a new book.

"When will I see you again?"

"Not for a while. I'm leaving tomorrow for a booksellers' convention. Not long after that, I'll be flying to Israel for two weeks."

"Let me go with you!"

"Oh, no," I protested. I steered him firmly but kindly toward the door and kissed him good night.

Watching his car disappear, I didn't know whether to laugh or cry. What a remarkable man. What had I thrown away? *Well, so be it,* I thought. *I'll probably never see him again.*

Although George could tell from my book that I had suffered, few suspected the secret agonies of my marriage, and I was too proud to show it. My husband, Lynn, and I lived "lives of quiet desperation" behind the façade of supposed success.

The truth was he could not show me the affection I craved. He was a fine man, highly respected, a model father, a manager of his firm. But the pressures of work were enormous, and as the years passed, he slipped into alcoholism. There is no loneliness like that of living with an alcoholic. Finally, in despair, I called our son Mark, who persuaded his father to go to Alcoholics Anonymous.

That blessed organization saved what was left of our marriage and probably Lynn's life. From then on, he had something to live for, and he was generous and giving. Fifteen years later, in 1979, he died.

It was April. George and I had been in constant touch by phone. I was thoroughly infatuated with him, but whenever he proposed I put him off.

At the airport before leaving for Israel, I was paged for a telephone call from Pittsburgh. "Before you go: W-Y-M-M? Translation: will—"

I broke in, laughing. "I get it, darling, but they're calling my plane. Tell you when I get back."

I had agreed to go to the shore with him on my return. And did. We spent glorious, carefree days swimming, dining, and dancing. I had already fallen in love with George's personality. Before our time at the shore was over, I was in love with something even more important—his mind. He was fascinated by so many things, and expressed himself with profundity and wit.

On Easter Sunday, our holiday was ending. As we sat in church, waiting for the service to begin, George reached for my left hand, and slid his own wedding ring onto my finger. He whispered, "I, George, take thee, Marjorie . . ."

Startled, I tried to quiet him. George proceeded, mouthing the words: "Will . . . you . . . marry me?"

While a few heads turned, I whispered, "Yes, oh yes!"

Thrilled, he called his family after church. "When?" they asked. "June," I heard him reply. "No!" I cried when he hung up. I had too many commitments that summer, I explained. "We can't possibly be married before Christmas."

"Christmas?" George gasped. "How could we endure being separated so long?" We had to, I insisted. We weren't a couple of kids. "That's exactly it," he said soberly. "We don't have that much time."

Three weeks later, George drove me to the airport. I'd promised my son and his family a visit. We were in tears at parting, but also cheerful and mature. We had so much to look forward to.

The next morning at Mark's house I was so happy I began dancing in the shower. Out of sheer exuberance I kicked as high as I could, then fell, crashing against the tub's rim.

The giving of love is an education in itself.

ELEANOR ROOSEVELT

For an instant I was in too much pain to think. An ambulance was called, and the four fractured ribs were taped. Worse, there was no call from George for the next three days. I was hurt, bewildered, and even afraid. What if his love was cooling? What if his family was advising him to think it over, urging him to wait? For the first time I realized how much I needed him.

Finally, on the third night, he called. Mark explained about the accident and handed me the phone. I was crying so hard I could scarcely speak.

"Darling, I'm so sorry!" George said. "I didn't want to bother you. I wanted you to enjoy your family."

"Let's not wait," was all I could say. "You were right."

"Thank God!" he said.

We were married on the Fourth of July.

As a young woman, I dreamed of marrying a man who would always be crazy about me. When things didn't turn out that way, I was bitterly disillusioned. Then I grew up and accepted some ancient truths: there are different *kinds* of love. There is romance, and there is devotion. Romance, we are warned, is fleeting. So we must settle down and be content. For years, I lived that way.

And then, George found me. In the ten years, six months, and eight days we had together—before he died of lung cancer in 1992—I had both romance and devotion, and I learned what happiness really was. As the groom was told at the wedding in Cana: truly, the best wine was saved for the last.

MY FAIR LADY

BY

OWEN CANFIELD

*E*very year, because Ethel put it in her budget, we piled into the station wagon, the dozen of us, and went to the country fair in Goshen, Connecticut.

"Remember," Ethel said. "Stay together. Don't touch the animals. We won't go on the rides today, okay? But later, a surprise."

It was 1968, and the baby was eight months old. Ethel pushed the stroller, and I rode herd on the other kids, ages two to eleven, as we took in the sights of the fairgrounds. There was so much to see, and we'd always stop to chitchat with friends.

Halfway through, Ethel steered to the shade of the chicken barn. Knowing what was coming, the kids clustered around her.

"Okay, who wants a hamburger?" As the cheer died down, she fished in her purse, counted carefully, and handed me a precise sum of money. "Take Kevin and Kathy and Steve and Sharon with you to help."

Then she handed Linda, the oldest, more money and said, "You and Sheila and Owen get the sodas. I'll take the little ones to see the chickens."

Along the way, I stopped and looked back at her, with her pink-and-white checkered shorts, white blouse, and tennis shoes. Even with her salt-and-pepper hair, she looked girlish. "Your mother's beautiful," I said to my charges.

Ethel would have frowned had she heard me. "You're a hopeless romantic," she often said.

We feasted and were again absorbed into the midway crowd, and finally it was time to go home.

"Do we have to go?" came the usual chorus.

"It's time," said Ethel. "We had a nice morning."

"What's our surprise? Are we going to get corn?"

"I've already got the corn. Who wants a balloon?"

Another cheer. She fished again, handed me money and said to the kids, "Go with your father," and to me, "Be sure you get different colors. Aren't the blue ones beautiful?"

I bought ten of them, amazed that she had budgeted for this too. Ten dollars was a fortune to us.

We ate sweet corn that night, and someone said, "Boy, did we have a good time at the fair." Two of the balloons had popped and one had floated into the sky, but for a day or two the others hugged the living-room ceiling.

Ethel was a genius at stretching money, but short-lived helium balloons seemed extravagant to me.

"Kids should have something to take home from the fair," she explained.

We returned every year to Goshen, and every year there were fewer hamburgers to buy. When the 1980s arrived, Ethel and I were going alone and calling it "a date."

Our best fair date was our last, in 1987. We were young grandparents, best friends anticipating the exciting decade of our fifties. The budget was not as tight. We had 32 years of marriage that had succeeded because each of us had put the other first every day.

Her hair was silver now. I had a paunch. Ethel reminded me that I should lose weight, but on fair day she indulged me.

I suggested that a pepperoni pizza would be nice.

"Owen, it's only nine o'clock in the morning!"

"A man gets hungry with all this walking in the hot sun."

"Oh, all right. You're starting too early though."

We walked the midway kidding and greeting friends. Then we watched the animal judging.

"You know, you still look great in shorts," I said.

"Oh, shut up."

"Well, you do." I took her hand and she said, "Owen, we're in our fifties." But she indulged me in this way, too, and we walked along holding hands as we had when we were nineteen.

"Look at that guy with all the muscles," she whispered. "He's flexing his biceps, hoping his girlfriend will see."

"Yeah," I said. "Basically, I'm built like that myself." She elbowed my ample stomach and laughed out loud.

We remained until early afternoon, and then she bought sweet corn. Some of the kids were coming for supper. When we drove off, I said, "That was the best date yet."

I put my hand on hers, and we drove along that way. Later, I wondered if she knew even then that she would be dead in less than a year. I believe she did.

The changes in seasons became difficult to endure without her. She had protected me with her perfect love. She never said, "Together we can make it." We just made it because we tried so hard. She never asked me to have a good heart. She had her own good heart and trusted me to

230

copy it. She didn't say, "I won't give up on you" when I was down. She just never gave up.

That first September after her death I sought to ease my loneliness at the fair. I went looking for peace, I suppose, but more likely looking for her. I walked the joyless midway, gagged on the food, and tried unsuccessfully to watch the cows being judged. This was our day, our fair. But she was gone. *What a mistake, coming here,* I thought.

I started to leave, walking rapidly, as if trying to outdistance the pain. Then I saw the man with the balloons. I stopped and stared at him, remembering.

"I'll take that blue one," I said finally.

The country cemetery was deserted. I tied the balloon to a basket of flowers fronting the handsome stone on which were engraved the words "Ethel Canfield, Beloved Wife, Mother of Ten."

Suddenly, a young father and his boy appeared. The child, perhaps three years old, had seen the balloon and become excited.

"Hello," I called. "Come over a minute." I snapped the string and put it in the youngster's hand. "From the fair. You like it?" Ethel would have wanted him to have it, I knew.

I drove off laughing, hearing her laughing with me. She was there in my heart, and I knew she would always be.

Gotta get some sweet corn, I thought. *Some of the kids are surely around, and we should have corn on fair day.*

HEAD OVER HEELS

BY

ANDREW H. MALCOLM

It all started because Hilde Vogel got hungry. The twenty-three-year-old secretary was visiting her brother's sixth-floor photo studio in New York City. He took forever to close. To save time en route to dinner, Miss Vogel summoned the elevator.

When the elevator door opened, she stepped in to pull the string on the light bulb. Oops! There was no elevator—just a black void.

Over at City Hospital, the call came in: woman falls down elevator shaft. The on-duty intern, needing a break, begged a colleague, Nathan Serlin, twenty-nine, to take that ambulance run. "It's probably a DOA," he said. "You'll be done in no time."

But Fortune smiled on Miss Vogel that day. It was only nine degrees out, and she had thick gloves on. She grabbed the elevator cable. She slid down. She landed hard, but not as hard as in a free fall.

It was Doctor Serlin who really fell. When he got there, she was "sitting on those stairs," he recalls. "Her hands were greasy and burned. But all I could see were those bright blue eyes." He also noticed no wedding ring.

Miss Vogel remembers two things. When the doctor bent down to examine her, his starched white uniform pants split. And he scrubbed her raw hands very hard to remove the grease.

Before releasing her, he noted her address. And two days later, being romantically unattached despite his mother's best efforts, he phoned to inquire if he might call on her. And she said the most amazing thing: "Yes."

Theirs was a simple courtship—long walks and shared gazes, 65-cent spaghetti dinners. One day he blurted, "How about marrying me?"

"What?" she replied.

One thing led to another, and here they are 53 years later sitting in their living room showing off photos of their two daughters and two grandchildren and reminiscing.

She recently reread the stacks of letters they sent across the Pacific during World War II. "He said he missed me very much."

"I still do when we're apart," he says, taking her hand. "And I still love that lady I met on those stairs."

LOVE BEYOND ALL UNDERSTANDING

BY

SUZANNE CHAZIN

On a chilly Friday morning in December 1992, the front-door buzzer sounded at Ken Rosenblat Electric, a modest storefront enterprise in Brooklyn, New York. Ken and his father, Herman, were preparing the week's payroll in the back office. "Somebody's in early," said Herman, checking the clock on the wall. It was 7:40 A.M. The firm's dozen or so employees weren't due until eight.

"I'll get it," said Ken. The thirty-two-year-old, who was built like a lumberjack and sported a reddish-brown beard, maneuvered his way through the warehouse, past boxes of switches and sprawling electrical cables. As he opened the steel door partway, he saw a young stranger fidgeting in the cold, his hands in the pockets of his down jacket. He was glancing nervously at a car gunning its motor nearby. In that split second, Ken Rosenblat knew what would follow. Too late, he tried to close the door, but the man pushed him inside, pulled out a revolver, and shoved its cold steel barrel to Ken's temple. "This is a robbery," the man said in a tight voice.

Ken pawed at the intruder's gun and pushed him against the wall. Surprised by Ken's resistance, the man relented for a moment. But when Ken relaxed his grip, the robber tore the gun from his hand and pushed him toward the back office.

The sound of the scuffle caused Herman to look up from his desk. Through the glass door of the office, he could see a man with a gun shoving his son. Panic rose within him, unlike anything he had felt since his boyhood in Poland.

"There is no money here," Herman told the intruder. "Please leave us alone."

Furious, the robber aimed the gun at Ken's side and fired. Pain sliced through Ken's body, followed by a cold, sweating numbness. His legs buckled, and he fell to the floor. *What will happen to Joanie and Michael?* he wondered, thinking of his wife and their six-month-old son.

Immediately, two more shots rang out, and Herman felt a burning in his stomach as he doubled over his desk. The robber shoved the gray-haired man aside, then grabbed the cash and vanished.

Herman clawed his way to the phone and dialed 911. "A man just shot me and my son," he said. As he spoke, he could feel warm blood dripping from his gut, but what terrified him more was seeing Ken's six-foot-two-inch frame lying motionless on the floor. *How will I tell Roma?* he wondered. *Have I survived everything for it to end like this?*

As Herman was lifted onto a stretcher, he felt himself drifting back to another nightmarish time. It was October 1942. He was thirteen, living in the Jewish ghetto in Piotrków, Poland. His father had died of typhus eight months earlier, and now there was a rumor that the Nazis wanted to ship the ghetto inhabitants off to a concentration camp called Treblinka. Everyone in Piotrków knew that Treblinka meant black-smoked ovens and certain death.

235

On a gray morning Nazi soldiers stormed the ghetto, ordering all its people to report to the marketplace. Two lines were formed—one for Treblinka, the second for work camps in Piotrków. Herman and his three brothers were directed to the work-camp line. Then the Nazis pointed his mother to the other line.

Herman raced to her side and threw his arms around her. If his mother was going to Treblinka, then so would he. He looked at her for approval, but instead she turned her head and spoke in a voice so hoarse and soft that he could barely recognize it. "Go away," she said, her eyes flooding with tears. "I don't want you anymore. You're a nuisance."

Herman stood in disbelief. His body, aching as if from a blow, folded into his brothers' arms as they carried him to the work-camp line. When he turned back, the line for Treblinka had moved on. He never saw his mother again.

Now, lapsing in and out of consciousness, he saw doctors leaning over him. "My son," he asked, "where is my son?"

"He's being examined," a doctor answered. "And we're prepping you for surgery."

Soon after Herman was wheeled into the operating room, his wife Roma, sixty, arrived at the hospital. She, too, was a Polish Jew who had lost family in the Holocaust. And she and Herman had also endured many hardships in their 34 years of marriage. There was the period when they worked opposite shifts—she, nights as a nurse; he, days as an electrician. There was the failure of an earlier business. Roma had a heart condition. Herman had suffered from phlebitis. And now this.

A nurse led Roma to a recovery room. Herman was still groggy from surgery, but just seeing him alive made Roma's heart leap. She slipped her hand in his and felt a warm, steady squeeze. He was with her again. That was all that mattered.

Herman's mind wandered back again, this time to February 1944. He was fourteen, a prisoner in a German concentration camp called

Schlieben, about 70 miles south of Berlin. His shivering body was emaciated, and he seemed but days away from dying of starvation.

One morning, dressed only in the paper-thin striped prison uniform, with his toes wrapped in rags, he looked out to the snow-covered fields beyond the barbed wire. Suddenly he spotted a Polish girl of perhaps eleven or twelve, dressed in a thick wool hat and coat, with oversized leather boots on her feet.

Dazed from hunger, he stared at her a long time. Instead of taunting him as others often did, she moved closer and spoke with a gentleness he had not known since he'd lost his mother. "Don't worry," the girl said. "You'll get out soon." Then she reached inside her coat and pulled out an apple and a piece of fresh-baked bread. "Here," she said, throwing them over the fence.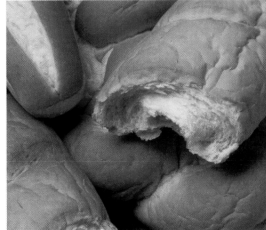

Herman looked around. The Italian guards temporarily in charge of the camp didn't police it as strictly as the Germans did. He grabbed the food and stuffed it inside his shirt. "I'll bring you more tomorrow," the girl promised.

Herman did not expect her to return, but the next day she was there with more bread and apples. Every day for seven months—until Herman was transferred to the Theresienstadt concentration camp in Czechoslovakia— the Polish farm girl came to feed him. Her hands brought forth a miracle. She gave him life.

"The surgery has gone well for your husband," the doctor told Roma.

"And my son?" Roma asked.

"It looks as though he'll pull through," the doctor continued. "But the bullet struck his spinal cord. It's unlikely he'll ever walk again."

Roma sank into a chair and burst into tears. The doctor's words cut to her deepest fear. She would always love her son, but would his wife?

From the first time she met Joanie, Roma doubted that she was the girl for their Kenny. She was more "American" than traditional Jewish in Roma's view. She was a modern, independent woman who didn't hesitate to speak her mind. She had lived alone and dated other men.

Joanie also enjoyed Ken's ability to earn a good salary. After they married, she and Ken traveled through Europe on their honeymoon, which seemed to frugal Roma and Herman an extravagant way to start a marriage. Roma and Joanie were always mutually polite, but neither had been able to show real warmth for the other.

These doubts had nagged at Roma, even though she could see Ken was deeply in love. Now Joanie often talked of buying a house. That would probably be impossible. Roma wondered whether their love would be strong enough to survive such failed dreams.

As Herman began to regain consciousness, Roma stroked his forehead. *I will not think of such things now,* she vowed. Then Herman groggily mouthed the question that had plagued his mind from the moment of the attack. "Kenny?" he muttered. "How are his legs?"

Roma swallowed hard, fighting back tears. Bad news could wait. "His legs are fine," she lied. "Now you must rest."

As she left Herman's room, she caught sight of Joanie walking briskly down the hall. She searched the younger woman's eyes for some sign that her doubts were unfounded. But in them she saw only her own fear and apprehension. "We're going to make Kenny well again," Roma blurted.

Joanie nodded blankly. What could she say? She was a nurse. The doctors had told her that Ken was paralyzed from the waist down. A part of their lives had died with that bullet. Gone were the beach and

True love's the gift which

God has given

To man alone

beneath the heaven.

SIR WALTER SCOTT

camping trips. Michael would never play football with his dad. The second child she dreamed of might now be medically impossible. And besides with Ken's income gone, Joanie would have to return to work to help support the family. She couldn't pretend these losses away.

Roma dabbed a tissue at her tears. "Don't tell Kenny or Herman about the paralysis," she pleaded.

Joanie blinked back surprise. "I won't tell Herman, if that's what you want," she promised. "But I always tell Ken the truth."

Roma waved her hands in front of her face. *How could Joanie be so cruel?* she wondered. Then a darker notion came to Roma. *Joanie is going to abandon him. That's why she's telling him the truth—to prepare him for her departure.*

Joanie realized that Roma doubted her. Still, she knew what Ken would want. "My parents always try to protect me and, given what they've lived through, it's understandable," he once told her during a difficult moment in their courtship. "But from you, Joanie, I always want the truth."

That night, Roma couldn't sleep. Every time she drifted off, she had nightmares of her son alone, without the woman he adored and the son he'd brought into this world.

Roma also kept recalling an old Jewish legend Herman had related to her in which, 40 days before a child is born, his spouse is selected in heaven. Two souls are created and an angel cries, "This boy for that girl!" From that day forward, no barrier can prevent their meeting, no hardship can alter the strength of their enduring love.

But what could Joanie know of love? Its sacrifices? Its hardships? Roma could not believe that, in all the world, the angels would pick this girl to stand by her son.

True love, Roma knew, bound two souls to eternity and turned them into one. Such a union could only be made by angels. For, surely, angels had brought Roma to Herman.

It was July 1957, in New York City, and Roma had agreed to a blind date, fixed up by her friend Sylvia, whom she had met through the local synagogue. Sylvia and her date, Sid, were going to Coney Island and invited Roma and Sid's friend Herman to come along.

Roma slid into the back seat of a 1955 Buick, next to a baby-faced young man with sparkling brown eyes that never stopped gaping at her. He was warm and funny. She liked that. He also spoke to her in the Polish accent of her homeland.

Gradually, they began to talk about their pasts. When he told her he'd been in the concentration camps, Roma found herself shuddering at the memory of the only camp she had seen firsthand. "There was a boy," she said softly, surprised that after all these years the memory still lingered. "He was in a camp near the fields where we worked. I used to throw bread and apples over the fence to him."

Herman leaned closer, his brow furrowed as if he didn't quite believe her. "What was the name of the camp?" he asked.

"I don't remember. It was in Germany, not too far from Berlin," Roma answered. "My father bought us fake passports that said we were Christians."

The young man's sparkling brown eyes became sharp and serious. "You fed him once?" he asked. Roma remembered feeling on edge. Who was this crazy man grilling her?

"I fed the boy for seven months. Then he disappeared. I feared the worst."

"And the guards," Herman continued, his voice cool and staccato, "were they German?"

Roma tried to put herself back in that painful moment in time. She saw snow-covered fields. She was snugly wrapped in a wool coat. Her feet were encased in oversized leather boots. The boy was tall, shivering in a striped prison uniform with rags on his feet.

"The guards wore some other uniform," she answered finally.

With those words, a dam broke inside Herman, a dam that had been building since that day in the marketplace in Piotrków. Gently, he reached across the seat and touched her hand. His dark eyelashes were wet with tears. "Those soldiers you saw were Italians," Herman said slowly. "I know, because I was that boy."

Roma shook her head in disbelief and looked into Herman's eyes with the kind of awe a blind person might feel glimpsing a sunrise for the first time. It was then she knew that the angels had picked her to be this girl.

On the third day after the shooting, Roma sat at Herman's bedside. She did not tell him about Kenny's legs. Instead, she plumped his pillows and told him he would get well soon. Herman smiled because his wife was at his side.

Later, Roma walked to her son's room and sank into a chair. Joanie was standing next to Ken's bed, pulling his mattress sheet toward her to roll her husband gently to the other side of the bed. He was soaked with sweat. Joanie took a warm washcloth and gently began to swab him.

The young woman worked silently, now and then reaching to squeeze Ken's hand reassuringly. Groggy from painkillers, he could do little more than grunt responses, but what struck Roma was how completely he trusted her, folding into her arms as willingly as a baby. Joanie's hands were giving Kenny life, just as Roma's hands had once done for her Herman years before.

As Joanie leaned forward at one point, Roma noticed something gold on a chain dangling from her neck.

"What's that you're wearing?" Roma asked.

"Ken's wedding ring," Joanie answered. "The nurses told me it might get stolen. I want to keep it close. That way, I'll always have a part of him with me, until he's able to wear it again."

Then Joanie walked over to Roma and patted her arm. "I want you to know that I didn't marry Ken's legs. I married Ken. I love him. I'll take care of him—I always will."

When Roma heard those words, she closed her eyes and fell into Joanie's embrace. These past few days, Roma had been praying to God to make her son whole again. She hadn't realized that, with Joanie's love, he already was.

According to the legend, there is a reason the angels proclaim a boy for every girl. It is the same reason that God gives man two eyes and two ears and two hands—so that they may work as one. Roma now knew that the angels hadn't erred in bringing her son and daughter-in-law together after all. They had worked their magic, as they had done for her and Herman.

All love is sweet,

Given or returned. Common as light is love,

And its familiar voice wearies not ever.

PERCY BYSSHE SHELLEY

ACKNOWLEDGMENTS

All the stories in *The Miracle of Love* previously appeared in *Reader's Digest* magazine. We would like to thank the following contributors and publishers for permission to reprint material:

Articles

Gold Touching Gold by Christopher de Vinck. "ONLY THE HEART KNOWS HOW TO FIND THEM," copyright © 1991 by Christopher de Vinck. Published by Penguin Books.

The Best Kind of Love by Annette Paxman Bowen. © 1989 by Annette Paxman Bowen. Focus On The Family (February '89).

The Dream Horse and the Dining-Room Table by Billy Porterfield. "DIDDY WAW DIDDY," copyright © 1994 by Billy Porterfield. Published by HarperCollins Publishers, Inc.

"You Will Have a Good Life" by Katharine Byrne. © 1992 by Katharine Byrne. America (November 14, '92).

A Love Like No Other by Skip Hollandsworth. © 1994 by Texas Monthly, Inc. Texas Monthly (February '94).

My Favorite Valentine by Chuck Thompson. © 1995 by Chuck Thompson. American Way (February 1, '95).

Wedding Tales by Robert Fulghum. From "IT WAS ON FIRE WHEN I LAY DOWN ON IT" by Robert Fulghum, copyright © 1988, 1989 by Robert Fulghum. Used by permission of Villard Books, a division of Random House, Inc.

Just Two for Breakfast by Marilyn Myers Slade. © 1994 by Marilyn Myers Slade. Yankee (February '94).

An Affair by Phone by James Lees-Milne. "ANOTHER SELF," copyright © 1970 by James Lees-Milne. Published by Akadine Press Inc.

The Loves We Leave Behind by Lisa Bain. © 1996 by Glamour. Glamour (March '96).

"Hello, Young Lovers" by Philip Harsham. © 1989 by Philip Harsham. St. Petersburg Times (October 4, '89).

My Husband's Hands by Helen Troisi Arney. © 1997 by Helen Troisi Arney. Chicago Tribune Magazine (July 20, '97).

Cauliflower Love by Erma Bombeck. "MARRIAGE MADE IN HEAVEN . . . OR TOO TIRED FOR AN AFFAIR," copyright © 1993 by Erma Bombeck. Published by HarperCollins Publishers, Inc.

A Story for Valentine's Day by Jo Ann Larsen. © 1985 by Jo Ann Larsen. Deseret News Magazine (February 10, '85).

For Better, For Worse by Robert Fulghum. From "MAYBE (MAYBE NOT)" by Robert Fulghum, copyright © 1993 by Robert Fulghum. Used by permission of Villard Books, a division of Random House, Inc.

Light After Dark by Edie Clark. © 1990 by Edie Clark. Yankee (August '90).

My Girl, My Wife by Charlton Heston. "IN THE ARENA," copyright © 1995 by Agamemnon Films, is published by Simon & Schuster, New York.

House on the Lake by Mike Royko. © 1979 by Chicago Sun-Times. Chicago Sun-Times (November 22, '79).

Love in an Unlikely Season by Marjorie Holmes. "SECOND WIFE, SECOND LIFE: A LOVE STORY," copyright © 1993 by Marjorie Holmes. Published by Doubleday, a division of Random House, Inc.

My Fair Lady by Owen Canfield. © 1990 by Owen Canfield. Northeast Magazine (September 23, '90).

Head Over Heels by Andrew H. Malcolm. © 1992 by New York Times. New York Times (September 29, '92).

Quotations

Ernest Hemingway, "A FAREWELL TO ARMS" (Scribner); *Douglas Stone,* "DIFFICULT CONVERSATIONS: HOW TO DISCUSS WHAT MATTERS MOST" (Penguin); *Anne Morrow Lindbergh,* "DEARLY BELOVED" (Harcourt Brace); *Joe Murray* in Maui News (April 27, '90); *David Viscott,* "HOW TO LIVE WITH ANOTHER PERSON" (HarperCollins); *Phyllis McGinley,* "THE PROVINCE OF THE HEART" (Viking Penguin); *June Masters Bacher,* "DIARY OF A LOVING HEART" (Harvest House Publishers); *Robert Frost,* "THE MASTER SPEED" (Henry Holt and Company); *Sam Keen,* "TO LOVE AND BE LOVED" (Bantam Books). Biblical Scriptures are from the "REVISED STANDARD VERSION OF THE BIBLE," National Council of the Churches of Christ in the USA (Thomas Nelson).

Photo Credits

All photographs are from Photodisc unless otherwise credited below:

Cover: Superstock, Inc.; title page: Koichiro Shimauchi/Photonica; pp. 2-3: D. Schwimmer/Bruce Coleman; p. 5: Birgit Hubert/Photonica; pp. 8-9: Raphael Macia/Photo Researchers; p. 11: Ann Cutting/Photonica; p. 15: Joan Slatkin/Bruce Coleman; p. 19: John Wilkes/Photonica; p. 21: Boden Ledingham/Masterfile; p. 23: Superstock, Inc.; p. 26: J. G. Edmanson/International Stock; p. 37: Kay Chernush/Image Bank; p. 41: Hulton Archive/FPG; pp. 46-47: M. Grondahi/Photonica; p. 48: Malabee Miller/Envision; p. 50: J. A. Kravis/Masterfile; pp. 52-53: Superstock, Inc.; p. 59: Novastock/International Stock; p. 63: Mark Bolster/International Stock; p. 67: George Matler/Envision; pp. 68-69: Meyers/International Stock; p. 70: Wayne Eastep/Stone; pp. 74-75: Superstock, Inc.; p. 77: Andrea Booker/Stone; p. 81: Florian Franke/Superstock; p. 83: Giovanni Lunardi/International Stock; pp. 84-85: Superstock, Inc.; p. 87: Hulton Archive/FPG; p. 88: Hulton Archive/FPG; pp. 90-91: Telegraph Color Library/FPG; p. 93: David Madison/Stone; p. 96: Joe Pollilo/Stone; p. 101: Feldman Lauree/Index Stock; pp. 102-103: Garry Hunter/Stone; p. 105: Andre Baranowski/Envision; p. 108: Superstock, Inc.; p. 110: David Woodfall/ICL/Panoramic Images; p. 121: Mary Teresa Giancoli; p. 123: Tim Davis/Stone; p. 127: Martine Mouchy/Stone; pp. 128-129: H. Horenstein/Photonica; p. 133: Andres Apse/ICL/Panoramic Images; pp. 134-135: Superstock, Inc.; p. 137: Superstock, Inc.; pp. 138-139: William Huber/Superstock; p. 141: Daniel Blaufuks/Photonica; p. 144: Fred Maroon/Photo Researchers; pp. 146-147: Solus Images; p. 149: Theresa Selye/Graphistock; p. 153: L. Doug Franga/Panoramic Images; p. 157: Richard Day/Panoramic Images; p. 164: John Ritter/Graphistock; pp. 166-167: John Wilkes/Photonica; p. 169: Stefan April/Stone; p. 173: Marvel Demmer/International Stock; p. 177: Ron Watts/First Light/Panoramic; pp. 178-179: Bruce Stewart/Bruce Coleman; p. 181: Dale Wilson/Masterfile; p. 185: F. Villa Flor/Photonica; pp. 186-187: George Lepp/Photo Researchers; p. 189: William Mullins/Photo Researchers; pp. 192-193: Wilhelm Schmidt/Masterfile; p. 195: Jonathan Safir/Photonica; p. 199: Scott Nielsen/Bruce Coleman; p. 205: Zefa Zeitgeist/Photonica; pp. 206-207: Jiang Jin/Superstock; p. 208: Pauline St. Denis/Bruce Coleman; p. 210: Cornelia Molloy/SPL/Photo Researchers; pp. 212-213: Steven McBride/Image State; pp. 216-217: Nigel Hicks/Superstock; p. 219: Pedro Lobo/Photonica; pp. 225-226: Garry Black/Masterfile; p. 227: Robin White/Photonica; pp. 231-232: Michael Gadomski/Photo Researchers; pp. 234-235: Photononstop/Envision; pp. 236-237: Tony Demin/International Stock; p. 243: John Slatkin/Bruce Coleman; p. 245: Raymond Forbes/Superstock

Carousel Research: Laurie Platt Winfrey, Van Bucher, Cristian Pena, Peter Tomlinson